ART AND HISTORY
SYRIA

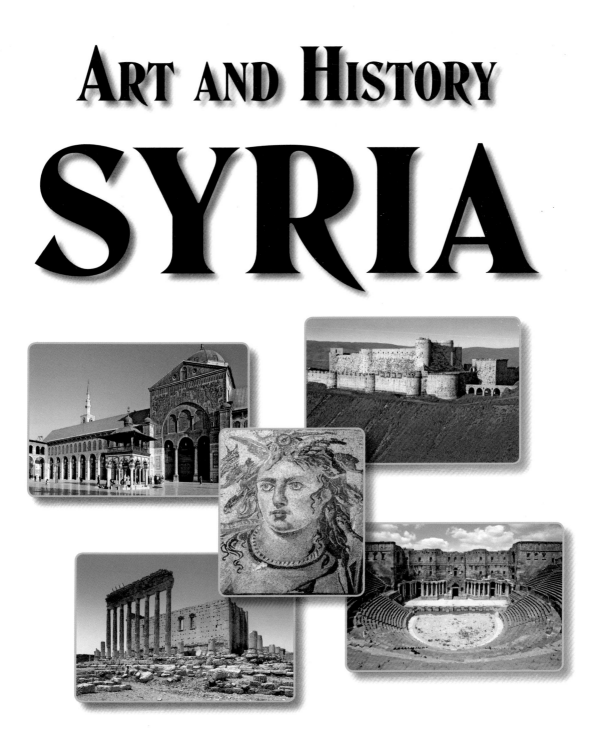

D0521548

EB
BONECHI

Managing Director: *Giovanna Magi*
Concept and editorial project: *Marco Bonechi*
Graphic design and cover: *Sonia Gottardo*
Editing and layout: *Elena Rossi*
Texts: *Francesca Casule*
Translation: *Paula Elise Boomsliter, Richard Dunbar*
Image research: *Giovanna Magi*
Map on pages 4-5: *Stefano Benini*

Printed in Italy by *Centro Stampa Editoriale Bonechi*.

The photographs are property of the *Casa Editrice Bonechi*
Archives and were taken by *Marco Bonechi*.

Other contributors:
Art Archive/Gianni Dagli Orti: p. 35, top.
© *Charles & Josette Lenars/CORBIS:* p. 87.
Andrea Pistolesi: p. 52.
© *2004. Foto Scala, Firenze - by permission of the Ministry for
Cultural Assets and Activities:* p. 7.

The photograph on p. 25, center left, was kindly supplied by
Vivaio Rose Barni, Pistoia.

The publisher apologizes in advance for any unintentional
omissions and would be pleased to insert appropriate
acknowledgements in any subsequent edition of this publication
if advised by copyright holders.

ISBN 978-88-476-0119-2

Internet: www.bonechi.com

INTRODUCTION

Due in part to the development of modern tourist facilities, Syria has become an increasingly popular destination for international travelers in recent years. As recently as 1986, only 20 percent of the 1.6 million tourists coming to Syria were from Europe, as opposed to the 55 per cent who arrived from other countries in the Near and Middle East. But in the wake of slackening political and religious tensions, the Middle East is drawing travelers who come to enjoy the area's rich historical, cultural and religious heritage. For these tourists, a trip to Syria will come as an authentic surprise: the souks of Damascus and Aleppo are among the oldest and most suggestive in the Arab world, featuring impressive architecture and high quality crafts, some of which—such as the fabrics and metals—continue to reflect great medieval traditions. In the main cities, visitors also still find the characteristic hammam (public baths); many caravansaries and patrician palaces have been restored and turned into museums; and entry is allowed in most of the mosques and other religious buildings, whose high artistic value and centuries, or even millennia, of history render them fascinating.

With the number of visitors enticed by various features of the Arab world growing in the last years, more and more people are coming to know the extraordinary wealth of the archaeological and monumental heritage of Syria. In

The city of Damascus in an engraving from Civitates Orbis Terrarum: the first volume was published by Georg Braun in Cologne in 1572; the sixth and last volume was published in 1617.

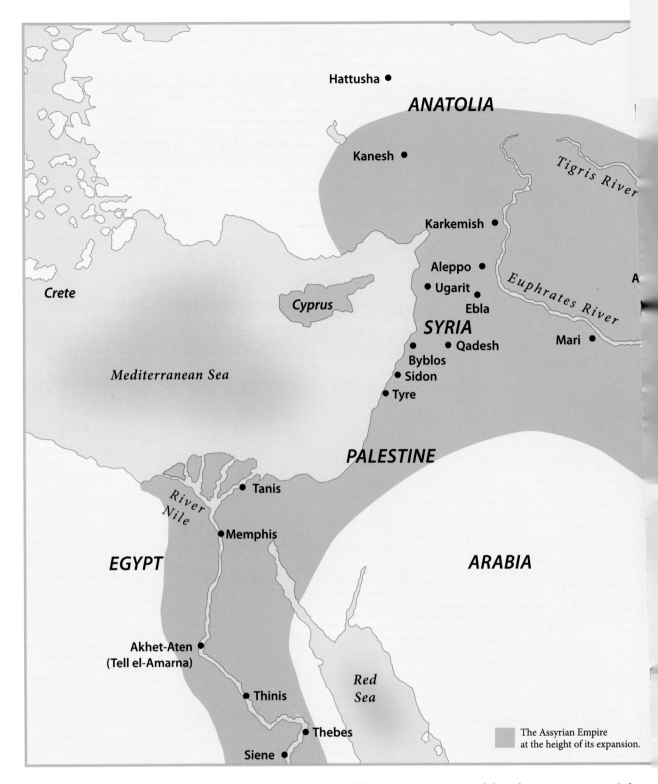

Hattusha •

ANATOLIA

Tigris River

Kanesh •

Karkemish •

Aleppo •

• Ugarit

Euphrates River

Ebla

SYRIA

Mari •

•   • Qadesh

Byblos

• Sidon

• Tyre

Crete

Cyprus

Mediterranean Sea

PALESTINE

• Tanis

River Nile

•Memphis

EGYPT

ARABIA

Akhet-Aten •
(Tell el-Amarna)

Red Sea

• Thinis

• Thebes

Siene •

The Assyrian Empire
at the height of its expansion.

reality, few places in the world provoke the emotions that one feels in gazing upon the ruins of Palmyra in the warm light of the sunset, surrounded by only desert and palms, or of first seeing Resafa and Dura Europos, whose great walls seem to materialize suddenly on the horizon. And what can be said of the miraculously almost-intact buildings of the dead Byzantine cities and of the basilica of St. Simeon the Stylite, where time seems to have stopped more than 1000 years ago. And how can we not remember Bosra, with its Roman theater with a huge frons scenae on three tiers, and the Decumanus Maximus, which

still preserves its original basalt paving stones. Other surprises await visitors to Apamea, which is reclaiming some of its grandeur as excavations and restoration bring to light an extraordinary colonnaded avenue, nearly two kilometers in length. Perhaps less spectacular, but of no less importance, are the ruins of Mari, Ebla, and Ugarit, as well as the many sites near the Turkish border and in the area of the upper Euphrates, where excavations in this century have uncovered entire "libraries" of clay tablets inscribed with cuneiform characters that provide keys for reconstruction of the early history of the Middle and Near

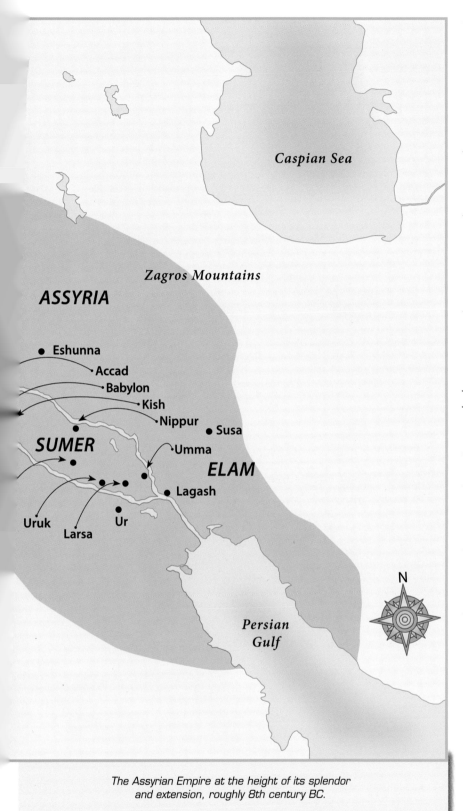

The Assyrian Empire at the height of its splendor
and extension, roughly 8th century BC.

Syria was the site of settlements as early as the Lower Paleolithic, with sites from hundreds of thousands of years ago found in the Anti-Lebanon, in the Orontes River valley and in the area of the Euphrates. Along the Euphrates, archaeological finds include stone tools used for hunting and skinning. These tools become more complex towards the Upper Paleolithic age, progressing to mortars made from basalt and naturalistic art objects in stone and fired clay at the beginning of the Neolithic. It was during this long period that the population passed from hunter-gatherers to a series of organized communities that produced food by cultivating grains and raising animals. The invention of ceramics allowed for the production of containers for storing food, just as the invention of writing served to record the quality and quantity of the goods in storage, which burgeoned thanks to abundant agricultural production. Between 3000 and 2000 BC, with the spread of metal objects, the area was further enriched. The production of these goods, first in hammered local copper, and then with tin and zinc to form resistant alloys, provided a first impulse to trade among geographically diverse areas, favoring the birth of large communities ruled by royal dynasties.

In the late 13th century BC, the relative balance between the Hittites and Ramses II following the battle of Kadesh (1293 BC) ended with the arrival of the so-called "Sea People," who, with a series of invasions, spelled the end of Hittite power and of some of the dynasties on the Syrian coast, including the rulers of Ugarit. The expansion of the Assyrians was in part slowed by the Arameans, a semi-nomadic Semite people who had moved into the Gezira and central Syria, creating a powerful reign with their capital at Damascus. In 732 BC the city finally fell to the Assyrians, who were however themselves swept away

East. Nor can we forget the dozens of castles spread throughout the country, the most important of which date back to the Crusader times and were strategically placed near the Mediterranean coast. Many of these complex structures extend over areas of several hectares, while some of the smaller castles, built in isolated areas overlooking rivers, in seemingly inaccessible gorges or on top of ancient ruins, are often no less suggestive.

first by a new Babylonian dynasty and then by another dynasty destined to overturn the balance of power in places as far away as the Aegean: the Achaemenid Persia of Cyrus the Great.

From 539 BC, the year in which the "King of Kings" entered Babylon, Syria saw its destiny join that of the other countries of the eastern Mediterranean: having become a province of the Achaemenid empire it was "liberated" half a century later by the army of Alexander the Great, remaining under the Greek sphere of influence for 250 years. Alongside the new cities, many centers of earlier origin were given new urban plans—in many cases still visible—which were in turn often enhanced by monumental structures built by the Romans after their conquest in 64 BC.

Despite pressure exerted by new dynasties coming to power in the East—that of the Parthians until 226 AD and then that of the Sassanians in Persia—the Roman province of Syria enjoyed relative stability for a long period.

The cities on the caravan routes, which maintained relative autonomy during the Roman aegis, especially flourished in this period. For those cities nearer the eastern boundary, however, the situation deteriorated in the second half of the 3rd century: with the destruction of Duro Europos by the Sassanians, Emperor Aurelian exacted a terrible revenge against Palmyra, whose population was decimated following a tumultuous rebellion.

In 395, with the division of the Roman Empire, Syria entered under the sphere of Byzantine influence, where it remained—with a brief Persian occupation between 590 and 629—until 636, the year in which the historic battle between the troops of Emperor Heraclius and the Arab army was fought on the banks of the Yarmuk River not far from Lake Tiberias. The Arabs, fired up by their new Muslim faith, crushed the adversaries, thus deciding the future of the area. Within only a few years, the Arabs had taken over much of the Near and Middle East, creating the basis for an enormous empire and relegating to their land of origin, Arabia, the role of an almost extraneous province.

In 661, with the rise to power of the first caliph of the Umayyad dynasty, the capital was moved to Damascus. With the rise to power of the Abbasid dynasty in 750, the center of power of the Islamic world shifted eastwards. The seat of government was transferred to Baghdad, the city expressly founded to be the new capital of the caliphate. Starting in the mid-9th century, a process of disintegration began that rapidly led to the division of much of Arab territory into small principalities. Helped by a religious legitimization of which no other sovereign could boast, the caliphs managed to formally maintain their hold on authority, as symbolized by the title of "Prince of the Believers." As early as the middle of the 10th century, however, the office was bereft of any real political meaning, and the capital itself had fallen into the hands of local dynasties, which held de facto power and established a sort of protectorate.

In this period, the areas of Syria and Palestine were wrested away from the Abbasids several times and made subject to dynasties in Egypt (Tulunids, Ikshidis, Fatimid. An important exception occurred between 944 and 10: with the Arab dynasty of the Hamdanids. In this perio Aleppo became the capital of an economically and cultu ally flourishing state, despite repeated conflicts with th Byzantine Empire and with the Fatimids who occupie the southern part of the country.

The Hamdanids and Fatimids adhered to different sec of the Shiisms, just as the Persian dynasty of the Buiyd who took over the power in Baghdad in 945, were Shiit With the Seljuks, who in 1055 substituted the Buiyds a "protectors" of the caliphate, the region witnessed th return of Sunnite orthodoxy as well as the emergence o the Islamic political scene of a Turkish dynasty, shortl destined to unite under its control much of the easter territory previously conquered by the Arabs.

With solid administrative organization and strong loca autonomy, the government of the Seljuks was accompa nied by a flourishing cultural and artistic environment Syria was not an exception, as it enjoyed a period of rela tive prosperity and intense building activity that was to continue even under the dominion of the Zengids, Turkish rulers who broke away from the Seljuks, and of the Ayyu bids. It was during the rule of the last Zengid, Nur al-Din, and of his successor Salah al-Din (Saladin), the first Ayyub sultan, that some of the most salient episodes of the wars against the Franks took place, as the latter made repeated incursions in Palestine in order to wrest away the control of the Holy Land from Islam.

The creation of a Latin Kingdom in the Levant by Geoffrey of Boulougne and his brother Baldovin during the First Crusade (1096-1099) was the fruit of collaboration between the armies recruited by the European aristocracy and the Pisan navy, aided by the other maritime republics. The Turkish reaction, however, was prompt: following the battle of Hattin (1187), in which Saladin defeated much of the Crusader army, Jerusalem, as well as almost all of Latin Syria, returned under the control of the Muslims.

Within the world of Islam, however, the balance of power was no longer the same: in the Near East, the Mamluks, Turkish slaves of Caucasian origins (from the Arab word mamluk, or "owned") called upon to form and direct the army, had assumed greater power during the rule of last Ayyub sultans, until substituting them in 1250. Alternating rulers of great and minor importance, the dynasty remained in power for more than two centuries, during which time both Egypt and Syria-Palestine underwent significant artistic and cultural development. Mesopotamia and northeastern Syria, however, fell soon thereafter under the rule of the Mongol Empire.

The Abbasid caliphs, fleeing their capital, found refuge with the Mamluk sultans, but their role further weakened. In 1401, a Mongol second invasion, led by Timur, not only brought further destruction to Baghdad but also pushed forward to Damascus, which was taken and sacked. The Mamluk rule over Syria was not threatened, however, until 1516, when a new and emerging dynasty in the Near East, that of the Turkish Ottomans, succeeded in annex-

TAMBERLANES ·
· IMP · ORIENTIS ·

TARTAROR
TERROR ·

*Timur the Lame, known as Tamerlane in the West, in a portrait by Cristofano dei Papi,
also known as Cristofano dell'Altissimo, who worked from about 1525 until 1605.
The canvas is now in the Uffizi Gallery in Florence, Italy.*

ing Syria and Egypt. *The Ottoman Empire, which already
held the entire Anatolian peninsula, expanded further
under Suleiman the Magnificent (1520-1566), spreading*

*from the Danube to the Tigris, from the Crimea to Yemen
and from Egypt to Algeria, coming to occupy almost the
entire Arab-speaking world as well as the last bulwarks*

Like any other great capital, Damascus has a modern, westernized side.
Important luxury hotel chains and high-fashion boutiques lend the city a contemporary air
that in no way contrasts with its millenary past.

of the Byzantine Empire. The almost four centuries of Ottoman rule in the Middle East saw immensely important transformations in the West as well as in the Muslim world. At the beginning, Ottoman control over the southern and eastern coasts of the Mediterranean undoubtedly favored Turkish commerce, but starting in the 17th century the supremacy of Europe became increasingly apparent.

In Syria, as elsewhere, the economic decline was accompanied by a sharp decrease in the population and farm production, as well as a stagnation, and even decrease, in industrial output, which was further crippled by shortages of water, minerals and energy. Despite this, the country continued to attract intervention: an attempted takeover by the Ottoman governor of Egypt, Pasha Mohammed Ali, led first to a short-lived separatist government (1831-40), and then—following bloody revolts and internal conflicts among religious minorities—to a regime of regional autonomy sanctioned by an international commission (1864) and guaranteed by Western powers.

This was the first step towards increased European meddling in the area. With the defeat of the Turkish-German axis and the definitive dissolution of the Ottoman Empire following the First World War, Syria passed under French administrative mandate (1920), and it was only after the Second World War, with the definitive departure of the French troops (1946), that the country became independent.

The ability to carry out stabilization and development policies, however, was strongly conditioned by the country's vicinity to Israel: for decades Syria was in fact one of the most active countries involved in the well-known Palestinian question. That resulted on the one hand in fragile political regimes, continually exposed to the shock waves of the Arab-Israeli conflict, and on the other to the need to invest in the military, which forced the country to live for many years in a war economy. The situation changed significantly starting in 1970, the year in which Hafez Assad came to power and began carrying out long-term policies for a planned economy.

DAMASCUS

*When Mohammed was asked why he did not visit Damascus,
the Prophet of Islam answered that one cannot go
twice to Paradise.*

Cited in Egyptian and Mesopotamian sources at the beginning of the 2nd millennium BC, the Syrian capital of Damascus is one of the oldest continually inhabited cities in the world. At the origin of this longevity undoubtedly lies the city's favorable geographic position, at the crossroads between the trade routes that since earliest times linked Egypt with Asia Minor and Mesopotamia with the Mediterranean Sea. Just as important was the presence of the Brada River, whose waters have allowed people to transform the desert into more than 9000 hectares of farmland for thousands of years. Almost nothing remains of the original city plan, which was the capital of an important Aramaic reign between 1000 and 700 BC. Instead, the outline of the regular city plan of the Greeks is still partly evident. The two areas were unified by the Romans, who surrounded the city with a circle of walls broken by numerous gates and enriched it with monuments, of which some vestiges still remain. The holy area, where initially the Aramaic temple dedicated to the god Hadda was located, was reutilized to erect the Temple of Jupiter and then substituted by a Christian ba-silica dedicated to St. John the Baptist. At the beginning of the 8th century, when Damascus was the political capital of the Arab world, the Great Mosque was built in the same area; to this day, it is the most important religious building in the city. Following a decline resulting from the loss of its role as capital, Damascus flourished again under the Zengids and Ayyubids, during which time the city spilled over the Roman walls. Numerous religious buildings arose from the heights of Mount Kassioun, which dominates the city from the northeast and provides the setting for the picturesque neighborhoods that still contribute to making the profile of Damascus particularly suggestive. After the terrible destruction brought about by the Mamluk invasions, the city expanded once again under Ottoman rule, spreading westwards towards the gardens flanking the Barada. Located in this area is the Tekkiye Mosque, built on orders from Suleiman the Magnificent and one of the most important religious buildings of the period. Also in this area are the large buildings built in more recent times which house the University and the National Archaeological Museum. Beyond the river, towards the north, is the modern center of Damascus, with its government offices and major hotels, while other modern urban areas spread out in all directions, pushed by rapid demographic growth.

THE GREAT MOSQUE

Despite the damage incurred by the Mongol invasions and numerous fires, it is impossible to remain untouched by this extraordinary building, built in less than 10 years by the Umayyid Caliph Walid I at the beginning of the 8th century.

The mosque occupies the entire area that once housed the *temenos* (sacred precinct) of the pagan temple, an area of enormous proportions, less than half of which is covered. The *court*, an integral part of Muslim religious buildings, stands out for its atmosphere of serene greatness, and the small pavilions located about it seem to emphasize, with the slight non-symmetry of their placement, the simple solemnity of the structure. But the vibrant suggestiveness of the *Prayer Hall* is unquestionable, thanks especially to the unique spatiality, at least for Western eyes, deriving from the placement of the naves, which are not longitudinal as in the classic plan of the Christian basilica but run parallel to the back wall. This design originates from the layout of the pre-existing religious building, whose longest side faced Mecca and therefore, in the passage of the building to Islam, was tapped to serve as the back wall. The solution must have proved functional and suitable for the needs of common prayer, and it was often repeated in the rest of the Muslim world, thanks also to the symbolic importance of this mosque.

The splendid courtyard of the Great Mosque of the Umayyad, with the fountain where the faithful perform ritual ablutions prior to prayer.

*Two views of the large courtyard and, right, details of the
Umayyad Mosque, in which polychrome marbles alternate
with intarsia of precious woods, superb mosaics,
richly decorated columns, and glistening brass.*

The Prayer Hall was rebuilt after the disastrous fire of
1893, in which the original wooden **shrine to St. John
the Baptist** was destroyed. The shrine was built on the
spot in which, during the demolition of the church, a relic was found that popular tradition has associated with
the Saint, who is also venerated as a prophet by Muslims.
Another attraction of the Great Mosque is the extraordinary **polychrome mosaic**, laid in 715 with the collaboration of Byzantine workers, but in an ideological
framework already fully Muslim: there is in fact no representation of living beings.
Mosaics originally covered the walls of the immense sacred court on both the sides of the arcades that enclosed
it on three sides, and the mosaics were particularly rich
on the facade of the main entrance to the prayer hall.
The decorations depict splendid idealized landscapes,
with buildings of several storeys, classical colonnades,
porticoes, and pavilions surrounded by rich vegetation.
The latter are made up essentially of large trees whose
green branches, represented in a rather naturalistic way,
move according to the shape of the walls. Festoons of
stylized flora decorate the small *octagonal pavilion* on

Corinthian columns in which the community treasury was once kept.

The Mosque was once covered by more than 4000 square meters of mosaics, but fires, earthquakes and other natural causes have reduced them to less than a quarter of the original. Over these more than 12 centuries, many attempts have been made to substitute the missing tesserae to recompose the unity of the design, but the results have not always been happy. The last major restoration, carried out with more modern criteria, took place in 1955: it was then that an attempt was made to recreate the polychrome tesserae with methods and ranges of colors to make them as close as possible to the originals, while highlighting the originals to preserve the historic testimony. The thin red stripe that runs along the perimeter of the section where the design has been integrated separates it from the areas that presumably date from the beginning of the 8th century.

On this page, details of the interior of the mosque, where the vast rectangular hall, 136 meters in length, is divided into three naves by two rows of columns on the first floor. The expanse of the south wall is broken by four mihrabs. Right, the small domed construction from the late Ottoman period is said to contain the head of St. John the Baptist, found during construction of the mosque. Islam considers John the Baptist a prophet; he is venerated under the name of Yahiya.

AROUND THE GREAT MOSQUE

Leaving the Great Mosque by the north gate, whose beautiful covering in bronze dates from the 14th century, you soon reach the small but interesting **Epigraphy Museum**, located in the **Madrasa Jaqmaqiya**, built at the beginning of the 1400s by a Mamluk governor. The madrasa, a school of theology including areas for teaching and lodgings for professors and students, was introduced in the 12th century by the Seljuk Turks in an attempt to strengthen Sunnite orthodoxy and then spread to the rest of the Islamic world. Among the first buildings of this kind in Syria were the **Madrasa Aziziye** and the **Madrasa Adiliye**, both dating from the end of the 12th century and located in the immediate vicinity of the Great Mosque. The first, built by the Ayyub sultan al-Aziz, preserves the remains of the sultan's father, the great Saladin, who died in 1193 and was originally buried in the Citadel. The second, with a splendid portal built slightly later, is today the home of the Arab Academy.

On this page, the entrance to a characteristic Turkish bath and the inner courtyard of the 18th-century Azem Palace.

Facing page. Top left, the Maktab Anbar, built in the 19th century; top right, a detail of the Nassan Palace, now used for state functions. Below, two images of the Nizam Palace, built in the 18th century and the former seat of the British Embassy, which boasts two beautiful courtyards and halls decorated with paintings and exquisite boiseries.

Another building situated in the same area is the **Madrasa Zahiriye**, containing the mausoleum of its founder, Baybars (1260-1277), the Mamluk sultan famous for defeating the Mongols and the Crusaders and winning for himself an important place in the history of the Near East. The funerary chamber was decorated with gold-base *mosaics* that copied, although with less skill, the decorative motifs of the mosaics of the Great Mosque.

Two other important buildings are found in the area to the south of the Great Mosque. The first, located between the silk market and the spice market, is another *madrasa-mausoleum*, in which the remains of Saladin's predecessor, Zengid Nur al-Din, are contained. The second, much more important, is the **Azem Palace**, the luxurious residence built in the mid-1700s by one of the Ottoman governors of Damascus, a member of the powerful Azem family.

The building was damaged by fire in 1925, but in the 1970s it was completely restored and transformed into the **Museum of Popular Arts and Tradition**. In effect, the Palace was from the start a collection of decorations and architecture taken from private homes and city monuments. A diary manuscript dating from the Palace's construction notes the owner's urge to collect the possessions of others, practically confiscating all that pleased him: mosaics, inlay, columns, arches, motifs of worked stone. He also demolished buildings of significant historical and artistic importance to build his own sumptuous residence a few steps away from the Great Mosque. The outcome must have undoubtedly impressed him: the Palace, today enriched by still more collections, has a very particular atmosphere. Also contributing to its fascinating appearance is the traditional division between the public area (*selamlek*) and the private area (*haremlek*), into which guests could not enter. The latter area includes a large *courtyard* with gardens, porticoes and fountains, a large *pool,* and numerous luxuriously furnished *rooms.*

THE OLD CITY

Although its predominant features are those typical of other Arab cities, the Old City of Damascus continues to show the strata of various eras and cultures. Its elliptic shape is in fact cut by the regular grid of the Greco-Roman plan, within which is the typical Islamic urban environment of narrow streets that branch out and terminate in dead-end alleys. This is less prevalent in the northeast section of the Old City, which has been inhabited for centuries by Christians. In this area, you can visit the **House of Saint Ananias**, where St. Paul was baptized by a disciple of Jesus and regained his sight. **St. Paul's Chapel**, to which another episode in the life of the Saint is ascribed, is situated nearby on the street that runs along the old walls. This quarter is also known for the picturesque antique shops found near **Bab Sharqi**, the only gate of the Roman walls to have survived to modern times, although altered during the Ayyubid dynasty. Starting at the eastern opening of the gate is 1.5 kilometer-long *Straight Street*,

cited in the *Acts of the New Testament* and acting as the main axis of Damascus during Roman and medieval times. Among the most interesting pre-Islamic traces are without doubt the large **colonnade**, which was part of the temple dedicated to Jupiter Damascenes built under Septimus Severus at the end of the 2nd century AD. The four monolithic columns, about 12 meters high and topped by a portion of pediment, also served as the monumental entrance to the church of St. John the Baptist, built under Emperor Theodosius I at the end of the 4th century.

The northwest corner is occupied by the **Citadel**, the enormous fortified structure which is currently closed due

Facing page, the House of Saint Ananias recalls Saint Paul's stay in Damascus.

This page, views of the interior and the austere exterior of Saint Paul's Chapel.

to works being carried out to transform it into a museum. Built by the Seljuks in 1079, it was almost completely reconstructed by the Ayyubids to resist possible attacks by the Crusaders. Containing a mosque, baths and apartments, the Citadel was the residence of the sultans during Mamluk rule, during which time it suffered two attacks by the Mongols. Taken over by the Ottomans in 1516, the Citadel was then used as a barracks and later yet a jail.

holy cities of Islam, Mecca and Medina.

His fame in the West was remarked even by Dante, who in the *Divine Comedy* placed Saladin in Limbo, "standing apart, alone," a great spirit ranking alongside the heroes and sages of antiquity.

In the photo on the left, the marble tomb of the great leader in the shade of the Great Mosque, in a building ordered restored by Emperor Wilhelm II of Germany after his visit to Damascus in 1898.

Facing page, several details of the rooms in the interior of the Citadel.

The entrance to the covered market is graced by the monument to the great leader **Saladin**, icon par excellence of Arab history.

Salah al-Din Yusuf ibn Ayyub (born in Takrit in 1138, died in Damascus in 1193) was sultan of Egypt and Syria and the founder of the Ayyubid dynasty. He governed energetically and wisely over Egypt, Syria, and Yemen and also controlled the two major

THE MARKETS

It is difficult not to be absorbed by the atmosphere of animated ferment that permeates the markets of Arab countries. As elsewhere, if not more so, the souks of Damascus are fascinating for their "variety," a term that refers as much to the goods displayed (fabrics and colorful clothes, household furnishings and wares, objects in copper, brass and other metals, spices, leather slippers, dried flowers, jewelry, wooden objects, candles, ribbons, sweets and ice cream, carpets, books, calendars) as to the people who come to shop.

Men, women and children dressed in western styles mix with people in traditional dress of all styles and colors, including the picturesque and ever-present licorice water vendors.

One of the most interesting markets is the **Souk al-Hamidiye**, a covered structure built along the south side of the Citadel in the section that was once the moat. Constructed in 1780, it was then rebuilt in 1863 during the reign of Ottoman Sultan Abdel Hamid II, after whom it was named. The souk can be entered from the western side of the Old City, while it provides the best point of entry to the plaza of the Great Mosque for those arriving from the modern city center. The tall lateral walls, into which the shops open, are covered by an arched corrugated metal roof. Huge lights and festooned light bulbs hang from the roof, adding to the lively and festive atmosphere.

Moving south, you will find another covered market, the **Souk Midhat Pasha**, at the western end of Straight Street. It was built in 1878 by the Ottoman governor after whom it was named and it specializes in traditional men's clothing. There are also shops selling herbs and traditional Arab medicines, displaying an array of products derived from animal and plant sources.

At the eastern edge of this souk is a cross street that runs towards the Great Mosque and is the location of the **Souk al-Bazuriya**, a picturesque spice market.

Festively explosive, a triumph of sensations, aromas, and colors: this is the world of Damascus' souks.

Coriander
CORIANDRUM SATIVUM

CHARACTERISTICS:
Annual herbal plant of
the umbellifer family. The
small sphere-shaped fruit
is incorrectly known as
coriander "seed."
IN COOKING:
Traditionally used in cooking
chicken and vegetables.
Ground coriander is used in
sweets, puddings and biscuits.

Cumin
CUMINUM CYMINUM

CHARACTERISTICS:
Cumin belongs to the umbellifer
family and is an annual herb.
It produces a fruit similar to wild
fennel seeds.
IN COOKING:
Cumin has a strong flavor,
characteristic of oriental
cookery. It is used in sauces to
accompany mutton and pork,
couscous, and vegetables.

Nutmeg
MYRISTICA FRAGRANS

CHARACTERISTICS:
From an evergreen
tree belonging to the
Myristica family.
The nut is found
inside a fruit not
unlike a plum.
IN COOKING:
Used generally to flavor
numerous dishes,
both sweet and savory.

Sesame Seed
SESAMUM INDICUM

CHARACTERISTICS:
The plant belongs
to the Pedaliaceae family
and is an annual herb
producing small pods that
contain seeds.
IN COOKING:
Much used in Chinese
and middle-eastern cookery
to flavour various dishes as
well as sauces.

The legendary **Rosa damascena trigintipetala** (the botanical name refers to the thirty and more petals that make up the double corolla of this flower) is not considered a species but rather a variety, an ancient hybrid developed through a thousand crosses among the roses of the Classical world, the favorites of the ancient Egyptians and Romans. Its origin is thus lost in the mists of time: some sources consider this rose, with its pink flower and unmistakable scent, to be native to India, but others place it in the Balkans whence the Ottomans would have imported it to Arabia. The modifier *damascena* (that is, cultivated in Damascus) recalls the medieval reputation of the roses of Syria, a country also known for its famous native son the physician and philosopher Avicenna, who among his many accomplishments is credited with developing the technique for extracting the scented essence from the rose petals. Even the ferocious Saladin held this rose in high esteem: it is said that on occasion of his conquest of Jerusalem (1187), he was preceded by 500 camels bearing Damascus roses to purify the city prior to his triumphal entry!

Many legends, one hard fact: the extraordinary scent of this rose and the essential oils contained in the petals have always had high market value, and a great many herbal products derive from it, from rose water to unguents, from perfumes to potpourris made of dried petals. The flowering of the Damascus Rose is typically short-lived, and thus no time is lost in harvesting its petals: the harvest begins every day at dawn and is completed by early morning, in a cloud of precious fragrance. Syria is still home to a culture centering on the ancient rose, which can be found in the secret gardens of Damascus, in the extensive fields where it is cultivated, and — transformed into an essence — in the souks for the delight of tourists. A curious fact: the rose essence is also used for scenting the water of the Turkish bath (or *hammam*) in an ancient rite of beautification and purification that may be followed by massages with rose oil, used for softening the skin and, it is said, improving circulation.

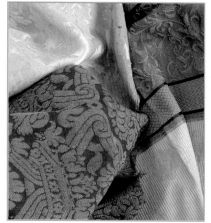

The weaving technique for this beautiful cloth, universally known as "**damask**," was invented in Damascus. Damask, used in women's clothing and decorating, is a handmade fabric, generally of a solid color with inclusion of brilliant threads, woven so as to create patterns in chiaroscuro relief.

THE NATIONAL ARCHAEOLOGICAL MUSEUM

A visit to the Syrian National Archaeological Museum will give you an idea of the country's extraordinary artistic heritage, which goes back more than 5000 years.

Even the *doorway* to the building is a masterpiece: the disassembled and then carefully reconstructed gateway of the Umayyad castle Qasr al-Heir al Gharbi, built by the caliph Hisham between 727 and 729. The semi-cylindrical *towers* are decorated in stucco with geometric motifs and stylized floral designs. The *reliefs* that decorate the gate's cornices are also exceptional, depicting shoots of vines, leaves and bunches of grapes among birds that emerge and peck at the fruit.

The museum is divided into six sections: **Prehistory**, **Syrian Antiquities**, **Classical Antiquities**, **Islamic Art**, **Contemporay Arabian-Syrian Art**,

One of the many clay tablets inscribed with cuneiform characters. The system for deciphering this difficult, complicated form of writing was developed by the German scholar Georg Friedrich Grotefend (1775-1853), although his key was later perfected by the Englishman Henry Rawlinson.

Right, a cuneiform tablet from Ugarit, with a legal text and a figured center seal (1300 BC ca.).

The decoration of a basalt fragment for ritual use shows armed warriors and lions on its sides and a banquet scene on the front. Dated to 1900-1850 BC, it was found in Temple B at Ebla.

Facing page, a seated female figure in alabaster, enveloped in the sumptuous, flounced ceremonial robes that were typical of the Early Dynastic III phase (2500 BC ca.), from the sacred precinct at Mari.

and the **Open-air section** installed in the museum's garden. Of special interest, the finds from Mari and Ugarit, dating to 3000-2000 BC, and the sculptures and paintings found at Palmyra and Dura Europos. The latter works are of fundamental importance for understanding the evolution of area art from the Classical canons to the two-dimensional, frontal perspective of the Byzantine period.

Although the collection of findings from the Greco-Roman period and of the first centuries of Christianity are not without interest, undoubtedly more unique for the Western visitor is the *collection of ceramics, glass, metal objects,* and *carved wood* from the diverse eras of Islamic Syria. The collections bear witness to the high artistic level reached in the Middle East when the West was still immersed in the so-called Dark Ages.

A bronze statuette of a god, originally laminated in gold (1300 BC ca.), from the southern urban area of Ugarit. The god, probably Baal, is shown standing in a warlike pose, his arm raised to brandish a weapon, now lost. Bottom left, a detail from a pitcher from that region of the mid-Euphrates region in which the Amorite culture developed. Bottom right, a deeply expressive, realistic portrait.
Right, the statue of Shibum, chief of the property registry at the time of King Iku-Shamagan. Shibum is shown wearing the kaunakès, with his hands joined in a sign of adoration, his head shaved, and inlaid eyes. Statues like this were placed in the temples by the faithful as votive offerings.

Facing page, this expressive ivory head of a prince (13th century BC) comes from the royal palace of Ugarit.

On this page, an elephant tusk carved to represent a nude goddess, with her arms crossed over her womb and an Egyptian-style sphinx at her feet.

Terracotta vases in the essential forms of stylized animals, from central Mesopotamia, the area in which the Turrite (or Khurrite) people, native to the Caucasus, settled in the early 2nd millennium BC.

Bottom left, the basalt statue of the Assyrian governor of Sukani Hadad-yis'i, from the 9th century BC. The skirt carries a bilingual inscription in Aramaic and Assyrian.

Left, the celebrated statuette of a seated figure from the temple of Ishtar in Mari which, thanks to an inscription, has been identified as "Ur Nanshe the Singer" of Ebih-il: the feminine cast of the features suggests that the subject may have been a eunuch.

Bottom right, the polychrome ceramic statuette of a horse and rider with typically Asian features. The statuette, from the Chinese zone of Turkestan, has been dated to the 12th century. The rider is shown fighting a dragon curling up the leg of his steed.

This page, right, a symbolic
representation of the Orontes river
in a mosaic distinguished by its formal
and chromatic vivacity.

Bottom right, a reconstruction of the
hypogeum of lahrai (2nd century AD)
from a tomb in Palmyra: the deceased,
surrounded by relatives, lies on the kliné,
wearing the tall headdress typical of the
priests of Baal.

Bottom left, this statuette of the
supreme god El enthroned and imparting
a benediction is 13.5 centimeters tall
and is dated to the 14th-13th century
BC. The statuette, from Ugarit,
is in gold-laminated bronze.

The facade of the mosque with its typical polygonal minarets; bottom, a detail of the ceramic panels, highlighting their incredible richness of color.

Facing page, a portrait of Suleiman the Magnificent.

THE TEKKIYE MOSQUE COMPLEX

In the immediate vicinity of the Museum is a religious complex built by Sultan Suleiman the Magnificent in the mid-1500s to host Dervishes (mystical priests who lived on charity) and pilgrims bound for Mecca. The building was designed by the Ottoman architect Sinan, the famous designer of many of the most beautiful mosques in Istanbul. The structure includes two rows of *cells* preceded by *porticoes*, as well as a kitchen and refectory, a *madrasa* and a **mosque**. The mosque has a prayer hall with a large cupola and two slender, tall minarets. Overall, the complex, with its rather sober decorations of stalactite motifs and panels of Turkish tiles, recalls other typically Ottoman buildings, and for this reason it was initially greeted without enthusiasm by the population. In recent times, the Tekkiye has been put to other uses: part of it houses the **Military Museum**, which is due to be moved to the Citadel when restoration there has been completed. Another section contains craft *workshops*

and *stalls*, constituting a sort of permanent exhibit of activities whose roots go back many centuries. This not-to-be-missed madrasa is an ideal complement to a visit of other craft markets: visitors can admire and purchase articles produced by traditional techniques, such as blown glass, embossed metals, and hand-woven damask fabrics.

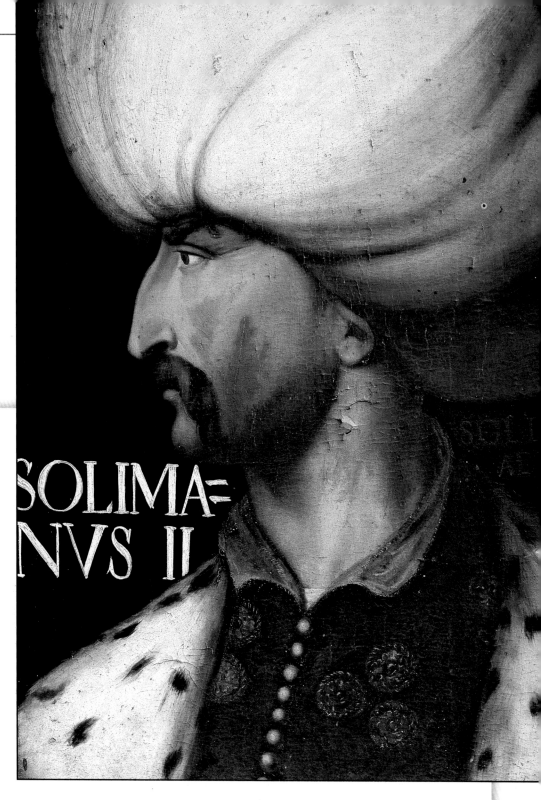

SINAN, SOLDIER-ARCHITECT

Mimar Sinan, Sinan the Architect or Koca Sinan, the Great Sinan, was born to a Greek Christian family in the Kayseri district of Cappadocia at the end of the 15th century. He lived to a very old age and died in Istanbul in 1588. Until 1514 he performed the military service required of non-Muslim youths from the Empire's various provinces. At the beginning of Suleiman's

reign he joined the Janissaries as a military engineer and participated in many of the sultan's campaigns: from Belgrade to Rhodes, from Budapest to Vienna, from Baghdad to Corfu.

From 1538 onward he devoted himself entirely to architecture to become the chief of the imperial court architects and, over the course of 50 years, served three sultans.

Sinan is considered the Michelangelo of Ottoman architecture, not only for the grandeur of his achievements but also for their number. He designed approximately 477 works, including 107 large mosques, mausoleums and madrashes, harems and palaces, tombs and chapels, aqueducts and caravanserai, and hospitals and fountains.

NEAR DAMASCUS

There are numerous interesting sites near the city of Damascus. A visit to the Shiite **Mosque of as-Sayyida Zaynab**, situated in the village of the same name a few kilometers south of Damascus, is worth the trek. The interior of the mosque, particularly rich in decorations, cannot be photographed and is accessible to women

On this page, a panoramic view of the village of Maalula and two views of the Monastery of Saint Thecla. On the facing page, bottom, an icon preserved in the Monastery of Saint Sergius in Maalula showing Sergius and Bacchus, Roman officials from Syria who converted to Christianity and were martyred in Resafa in the late 3rd century.

only if they are covered with a robe from head to toe.

The Christian villages of **Maalula**, **Seidnaya** and **Yabrud** in the Anti-Lebanon mountains are also of great interest. Maalula, in addition to its monuments and picturesque landscape, holds claim to a unique feature: the population still speaks the ancient Syriac dialect, which is to say the language, called Western

Aramaic, in which Christ spoke and in which some books of the Old Testament were written. The village is tightly linked to the history of Saint Thecla, the young pagan converted by Saint Paul. A Greek Orthodox convent is dedicated to the saint in the place where she was said to have found permanent refuge. According to the legend, the mountain miraculously opened, creating the narrow gorge in the upper part of the village that allowed the girl to escape from her persecutors.

Above, the Monastery of Our Lady of Seidnaya resembles a fortress, surrounded as it is by high walls. One of the chapels in its interior is home to a miraculous icon of the Virgin.

37

Driven by the river current, the norias of Hama have turned since the Ayyubid era to irrigate the countryside surrounding the city.

HAMA

Hama is another of the Middle Eastern cities that have been continually inhabited for millennia and are therefore extraordinarily rich in history and ancient traditions. Probably founded around the 5th millennium BC, Hama flourished during the 2nd millennium when it was the capital of an Aramaic dynasty of Syro-Hittite culture; subsequently, it was ruled by the Assyrians, the Persians, and then the Macedonians.

A relative decline occurred during Roman and Byzantine times, while the city's entry into the Islamic world (638) marked a new period of prosperity, as can been seen in the large number of ancient religious buildings. One of the most interesting and best conserved is without doubt the **Al-Nuri Mosque**, built on the right bank of the Orontes in 1170, during the Zengid era. The splendid wooden pulpit inside of the mosque is from the same period.

About a century and a half later, the **Abu al-Feda Mosque** was built. The mosque houses the mausoleum of its founder, a famous Arab historian and geographer who was the governor of Hama for many years.

The ancient monuments in the city, which is still charac-terized by only partially modified medieval architecture, include numerous *public baths* built between the 12th and 19th centuries, a *hospital*, a *prince's residence*—which now houses the **Archaeological and Folklore Museum**—and several *caravansaries*. These latter struc-tures—common in all centers of trade in the Middle East—responded to the need to provide lodging to mer-chants and pilgrims and areas for stabling animals and storing merchandise. Hama had some 30 caravansaries, some of which, especially those from Ottoman times, are still in good condition.

The special attraction of the city, however, is something else: among the traditional buildings and handsome monuments, you can still see the giant **wooden water-wheels**, or **norias**, used until a short time ago to draw and distribute water from the Orontes to the city. At present, they are still put to use for several months a year, but with the sole purpose of maintaining the traditional image of the city.

AZEM PALACE

This splendid 18th-century Ottoman residence was built by the Pasha of the wealthy and powerful Azem family, which also owned the famous palace in Damascus. As

in Damascus, the palace at Hama has numerous areas reserved to make the lives of the women comfortable but separate from the men, as was once tradition in the Islamic world. After a long restoration, the building has been reopened to the public, who can admire traditional *furnishings* and *decorations*—enlivened by statues in period dress, traditional in Middle Eastern folklore museums—as well as *collections of archaeological finds* from the area of the citadel and the entire region of Hama. Of special interest is a finely made **mosaic** depicting women musicians.

THE NORIAS

Of the many expedients devised by the Arab world to draw and distribute water, the noria is certainly the most spectacular. This is especially true when, as along the Orontes River, these wooden wheels are of colossal dimensions, becoming an integral part of the landscape in which they are placed. Particularly suggestive are the

Three images of the Azem Palace. Here, as in all the Syrian palaces, the private spaces were cleanly separated from the public areas.

The Azem Palace museum's most important holding is the very large (380 x 278 centimeters) **Mosaic of the Musicians** that decorated the floor of the *triclinium* of a villa in the village of Mariamin. The style of the figures, the gravity of the expressions, and the frontal representation of the faces with large, wide-open eyes, is an extraordinary precursor of the early Byzantine manner. The mosaic represents six musicians: crotalum players, the organist, the flautist, the percussionists (in the photo below), and a lyre player and dancers with castanets.

sound produced by their incessant turning, a screeching and creaking that permeates the city, and the sight of the tiny beads of water seemingly held in suspension. There are still 16 norias in Hama, half the number that once existed, and almost all of them date back to the late Middle Ages.

They are usually found in clusters, although each has its own name. Only the *Al-Mohammediyeh noria*, with its diameter of 21 meters, making it the highest in Hama, stands alone and dominates the western section of the city. The discovery at Apamea of a mosaic from the 5th century AD depicting a large vertical wheel has confirmed the hypothesis that the these structures have been present in the area since remote times.

AROUND HAMA

In addition to Apamea, the area surrounding Hama offers numerous attractions, including important traces of the Byzantine civilization that preceded the Arab conquest.

Heading southeast out of Hama, you come upon the Arab fortress of **Qalaat Shamamis**, built around the crater of an extinct volcano, and then **Salamiya**, a small town of Byzantine origin subsequently populated by a community of Ismaili Muslims.

Northeast of Hama are some picturesque villages inhabited by farmers and herdsmen, whose conical mud houses vaguely recall the *trulli* houses of Puglia in southern Italy. This is the case of the village of **Tayyebat at-Turki**, with its suggestive cemetery containing white tombs, on the road to the spectacular ruins of **Qasr Ibn Wardan**.

APAMEA

It is difficult not to be taken in by the fascinating contrast between the airy and opulent vestiges of the ancient Hellenistic city of Apamea and the bleak medieval village of **Qalaat Mudig**, perched on the hill where the acropolis once stood.

The discovery of cut paving stones, funerary objects, and ceramic fragments, as well as a Hittite stele, attest to the presence of a stable population since Neolithic times, but the founding of the city called *Apamea* is attributed to Seleucus I around 300 BC. As the main city of the Tetrapolis of Syria (which included Antioch, Seleucia, and Laodicea), Apamea maintained its importance after the Roman conquest (64 BC), but was practically razed to the ground by an earthquake in 115 AD. Entirely reconstructed in the 2nd century, Apamea was given a monumental plan which is still clearly legible in the surviving vestiges, including the **colonnaded avenue** (corresponding to the cardus), 1850 meters long. The seat of a neo-Platonist school of philosophy and of an oracle linked to the temple of Zeus Belos who enjoyed fame throughout Syria, the city preserved its classical and pagan cultural heritage for longer than other cities, even though it had been made a bishopric with the Edict of Constantine. By the end of the 4th century, Apamea was nonetheless fully Christian and had numerous churches, which still remained in use

for centuries after the Islamic conquest. The situation changed suddenly at the beginning of the 12th century, when the city was taken by the Christian Prince Tancred, but was then conquered in 1149 by the Zengid Sultan Nur al-din. Adding to the latter's reprisals were two dramatic earthquakes that destroyed the lower city. The surviving population took refuge on the hill of the acropolis, which the Zengid sultan fortified, giving it the picturesque, if bleak, appearance that it still maintains today.

THE COLONNADED AVENUE

The cardus of the city of Apamea was undoubtedly one of the longest colonnaded avenues of the ancient world. The width of the avenue was also exceptional, measuring more than 22 meters, or more than 37 meters if the porticoes that flanked it are included. Its construction probably proceeded from north—where the ruins of the **Antioch Gate** still lie—to south, in the direction

change from classical architecture. Another analogy can be found in the desire, in both cities, to differentiate different tracts of the main avenue, avoiding a long perspective view, which, although monumental, could also be monotonous. At Palmyra, the idea is taken to extremes through a number of sudden changes of direction in the avenue itself. At Apamea, a refined compromise was instead chosen: the cardus was divided into sections, separated by two votive columns and a tetrapylon, with the column shaft of the lateral porticoes designed differently. The designs include smooth or fluted columns (or with a convex element that fills, up to a certain height, the concave parts of the fluting); of great effect, for the splendid play of light that they create, are the spiral fluted columns. Also unforgettable are the smooth columns with bulb-shaped bases that made up the monumental facade of the **agora**.

The agora, with its rather unusual long shape (about 45 by 300 meters), was lo-

of Emesa (Homs), and it is in this same direction that the excavations and restoration of the city, for centuries scattered in and beneath the earth, are taking place. The work has been carried out by the Syrian Antiquities Department since the end of the 1980s (before that only a short length of portico had been recovered by a foreign team), and it should in a relatively short time restore the grandeur of Apamea. As in Palmyra, some of the columns feature inscribed corbels, a detail that represents a

cated at the southern section of the city. Seeing the pavement of the Agora can provoke a certain effect, as it is still uneven and distorted as if the earthquake that destroyed Apamea had just occurred.

The vestiges of the pagan city include the **Tychaion**, a temple erected in honor of the Goddess of Fortune, as well as some *baths* (the best preserved is to the north), a few remains of the *nymphaeum* and the barely legible structure of an enormous *theater* (the largest in Syria),

On these and the preceding pages, images of the columns that make the fame of Apamea, one of the ancient world's most celebrated cities. The columns are lined up over two kilometers in two parallel rows, about forty meters apart. Such famous philosophers as Posidonius and Numenius lived in Apamea; in the early 4th century, Jamblicus directed the neo-Platonic school here.

which was unfortunately used for centuries as a source of building material.

Interesting, although in a worse state of conservation than elsewhere, are the Byzantine ruins, located mostly around the area of the decumanus. The decumanus itself, which departs from the colonnaded avenue after the nymphaeum, is partly paved with asphalt because it was used as an access road to the ruins.

Among the most interesting vestiges is the **Cathedral**, originally conceived with a central four-foiled plan following the design of a martyry (in fact, a relic of the Cross was kept there). Some additions and modifications were carried out on the original 5th-century building in the subsequent century, when the adjoining episcopal complex became one of the most important of Eastern Christianity. The **floor mosaics** found in this area, dating to different periods, are of great importance. The subjects range from the complex Neo-Platonic symbolism of the representations on the lower levels, at-

tributable to a 4th-century non-Christian building, to later works, no less magnificently crafted, reflecting the themes of the dogmatic disputes that divided the Christian world at the time.

Only a few ruins remain of the so-called **circular church**, dating from the 6th century and situated at the intersection of the cardus and decumanus. The church was a large hall with a central plan and was preceded by a porticoed court.

Continuing towards the south, on the east side of the decumanus, you come to the vestiges of a **church and atrium**, probably built during the reign of Justinian on an earlier construction. The church conserved several relics of Saints Cosmas and Damian, which remained objects of great veneration in all of Syria even long after the Islamic conquest, as the numerous dated burial sites in the area attest. Kept in reliquary boxes with a funneled opening and an exit hole, the relics were meant to "sanctify" oil that was poured through the box.

THE MUSEUM

Excavations in Apamea began in the 1930s. After they were halted, the digs were taken up again for a short time in the 1960s by a Belgian team, and then in the last decade by Syrian authorities on a more regular basis. The various excavations have uncovered numerous objects and mosaics of remarkable quality, now found in museums in Brussels, Damascus, Hama, and Apamea. In Apamea, the findings are exhibited in an Ottoman caravansary located near the medieval village and recently restored by the Syrian Antiquities Department, which has confronted with spirited enthusiasm the difficulties and hardships of unearthing and restoring the city. The building, constructed in the 16th century as a stopping point for caravans, is a characteristic structure with barrel-vaulted spaces set around a central court. The **museum**, opened in 1982, includes a small section dedicated to folklore, but of greatest interest are the **mosaics**. Particularly striking are the *Portrait of Socrates among the Knowledgeable* and the *Victory of Cassiopea over the Nereid*, both of which are attributed to the 4th century and were found in the area of the cathedral. Their refined craft clearly shows their derivation from the Hellenistic tradition, although some later examples, characterized by stylization with roots in the Roman tradition, are no less pleasing.

Top, the twisting ribs of the columns of Apamea (mid-2nd century AD).
In the other images, rich mosaic decoration speaks of the luxury of Apamea's private homes and of how Greek culture had imbued the higher strata of Syrian society of the times.

ΓΕΟΡΓΙΣΚΛΑ

THE DEAD BYZANTINE CITIES:
MAARAT AL-NUMAN

The land to the northwest of the highway between Hama and Aleppo witnessed extraordinary development in the first century of Christianity, leaving great cathedrals, more or less in ruins, scattered about the landscape as well as numerous "dead Byzantine cities," abandoned after the Arab conquest and still often surprisingly intact after well more than a millennium.

In fact, many of the buildings, although without roofs, were constructed with perfectly square cut stone and still preserve their original decorative motifs.

To form an idea of the refined culture that characterized these towns, you should first stop in the town of **Maarat al-Numan**, home since 1987 of an interesting **museum** displaying findings from the entire region.

The collections, housed within a large 17th-century caravansary—the **Khan Murad Pasha**—include ceramics (from antiquity to the Islamic era), glass, metal objects and weapons, as well as mosaics and architectural elements in sculpted basalt, all found in the Byzantine cities of the area. The inevitable section dedicated to folklore occupies an entire wing of the spacious building.

The so-called "Photios mosaic" portrays numerous animals, both domestic and wild, with an unusual freshness of line and a great naturalistic sense.

SERJILLA

A different sensation is provoked by the vestiges of the city of Serjilla, which emerge in a somewhat spectral fashion in the middle of barren red earth littered by stones. Particularly suggestive is the view from above, where the **necropolis** extends in a series of *stone sarcophagi*, decorated in relief, that usually conceal a tomb or hypogeum.

The treeless landscape allows you to take in the entire extension of the city, in which numerous villas and churches can still be easily recognized. Among the best preserved buildings are the **baths** and a nearby structure whose front is preceded by a double-rowed portico that according to recent studies might have been an inn and a gathering place.

Most of the buildings have lost their roofs, but the rest of the architectural elements are in a good state of conservation. Where the floors of the lower stories are still intact, the rooms are used occasionally as pens for animals.

On this and the following pages: images of Serjilla, north of Apamea, a fine example of a Byzantine village that experienced a moment of prosperity in the 6th century. The building stones of Serjilla are accurately dressed; the facades of the churches and homes are engraved with many Byzantine crosses.

Bara

Set amid olive trees, many of the ruins of Bara, the largest of the dead Byzantine cities, emerge nearly intact from the warm ochre-colored earth. Among the most suggestive and best preserved buildings are the monumental *pyramidal tombs*, with a cube base, decorated with protruding moldings and cornices and surmounted by a pyramid-shaped cover of cut stone blocks with a small external corbel. The corbel, in addition to producing a pleasing decorative effect, probably had a functional use: it has in fact been hypothesized that candles were placed on them during funerals and commemorations for the dead.

Also found in the area are *hypogea*, or underground tombs, and two-storey villas, sometimes fronted by a portico, as well as three churches with three-nave basilica plans.

Different from what happened at most of the other sites, Bara was not suddenly abandoned and the city continued to be inhabited for several centuries following the Arab conquest, with the new populations coexisting. This is demonstrated by the presence of several antique Muslim tombs and the reference to the conquest of Bara by the Crusaders between 1098 and 1123.

An arch and one of the two monumental tombs at Bara, suggestively set among olive plantations.

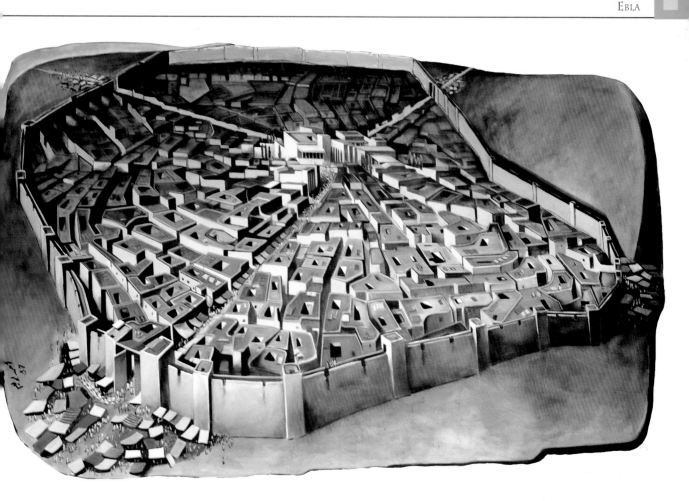

A scale model of Ebla showing how the entire area of the ancient Tell Mardikh was encircled by a bastion of packed earth, still very well preserved today: in the circle of walls, topped by fortified walkways, there opened four gates, one of which onto the road to Aleppo and another toward Damascus. Bottom right, a room in Palace Q (or West Palace) where grain was ground for bread-making.

EBLA

The highway running north to Aleppo crosses a region of steppes, with fields of grain stretching out in all directions. At the beginning of summer, the roads are traversed by trucks and other vehicles picking up seasonal workers for the harvest: colorfully dressed young women bring a festive note to the groups of workers who toil under the baking sun. The dropping-off points of the harvest, where the sacks of grain are stacked and inspected upon delivery, are a unique sight. Here, the amassed bags seem to form cities, with streets and passageways running between the mountains of sacks, all stacked regularly one on top of the other until they seem to form buildings.

It was probably the richness of the soil, together with the strategic position of the area, that ensured the fortune of the city of Ebla, whose remains emerge in the site at

*On the facing page, a detail of the famous Royal Archives of Ebla
and a view of the palace's dye-works. This page, an oil press and a large stone jar.*

Tell Mardikh, situated about 30 kilometers northeast of Maarat al-Numan. Although undoubtedly less spectacular than most of the other archaeological sites in Syria, the vestiges of Ebla are of extraordinary importance and probably constitute the 20th century's most relevant archaeological discovery in the Middle East. The discovery is attributed to an Italian team from the University of Rome, led by Paolo Matthiae, who since 1964, in collaboration with the Syrian government, has dedicated himself to the systematic excavation, study, and restoration of the many findings uncovered in the site.

The city, which was already flourishing in the 3rd millennium BC, was sieged for the first time by the Akkadians. Paradoxically, the destruction of the enemy city allowed its memory to survive: the *clay tablets* kept in the Royal Archives were actually preserved in the fires that were meant to destroy them, giving scientists a remarkably complete picture of the antique urban center.

Ebla was subsequently destroyed and rebuilt several times before being definitively abandoned around 1600 BC when the area was conquered by the Hittites.

The site is spread over a broad hill covering some 60 hectares, half of which house the *acropolis*, still protected on its eastern flank. The massive perimeter *walls* of the city, built in earth as are most of the buildings, are as high as 20 meters in some points.

Of the four *gates* that passed through the walls, the best preserved southwest section still maintains its stone footings. But the remains in the best state of conservation are those of the **Royal Palace**, with its numerous rooms and stone staircase.

It was in this area that thousands of tablets were found, from which it was possible to obtain precious economic, administrative, and legal information. The excavations carried out in the areas of the acropolis and lower city have led to the discovery of other palaces and religious buildings as well as an extremely rich variety of objects, often made of precious materials and with elaborately engraved and hammered decorations, and of statuettes and cylindrical seals. These finds have contributed to making a visit to the Syria's major museums more inviting than ever.

IDLIB MUSEUM - EBLA

The majority of the objects found in Ebla are now on exhibit at the **museum** in Idlib, a small city in northwest Syria, the capital of an important governorate. Today, the city is well known for its production of olives and olive oil, wheat, cotton, and fruit—and cherries in particular. The historical importance of Idlib is testified by the presence of many *tells*: more than 190 in number, the tells are the result of thousands of years of urban stratification.

The digs at Ebla have yielded up a great number of pieces of *pottery*, many of which are zoomorphic in form.

One of the 17,000 cuneiform tablets engraved in archaic Semite (later dubbed "Eblaite" by scholars), whose discovery represented an important contribution to the study of Oriental history. The texts are administrative, religious, economic, historic, and legal in content and were divided by subject. The clay tablets are of various sizes, from large and square (up to 45 cm per side) to smaller and circular.

ALEPPO

"It is with a sentiment of joyous stupor that one draws near to Aleppo,"
wrote J. Sauvaget at the beginning of the century, alluding to the sudden and unexpected
appearance—after hours of crossing a flat and barren landscape—of the city's expanse of roofs
and minarets, surrounded by green and topped by the imposing mass of the citadel.

Aleppo is in effect one of the most fascinating cities in the Middle East, and the wealth and variety of its attractions should come as no surprise, considering that it is one of the world's oldest continually inhabited places.

Remembered as the capital of the powerful kingdom of Yamkhad in 1780 BC, Aleppo then passed under the rule of the Hittites, who temporarily lost control when the city fell under the influence of the Hurrites and Egyptians. After the devastation caused by the invasion of the Sea Peoples, the city once again flourished as the capital of a Neo-Hittite state, which in subsequent centuries attracted the attentions of the Assyrians, Babylonians, Medes, and Persians. Following conquest by Seleucus I Nicator at the end of the 4th century BC, the city was named *Beroia* and given a new regular grid street plan which can still be recognized in the area to the east of the Antioch Gate.

Obscured by the importance assumed by nearby Antioch, the city lost political and economic clout during Greek and Roman times. Aleppo slowly regained some of its importance with the Islamic conquest, and by the 10th century it once again flourished under the Hamdanid dynasty, during which time the original plan of the Citadel came into being. It is however to the Zengids, and especially to Sultan Nur al-Din, that the city owes much of its present appearance: it was then that the walls, the Great Mosque founded by the Umayyads, and the famed covered markets were rebuilt, and numerous Koranic schools were founded. The Citadel received its present look under the Ayyubids, who dug the moat and shaped the escarpment that still surrounds much of it. The devastation wrought by the Mongols in 1260 inflicted a hard blow to the city, which nevertheless managed to rise up again in a short time. This is demonstrated in detailed descriptions from the end of the 13th century that enumerate more than 700 mosques, schools, public baths, and hospitals.

With the Mamluks, Aleppo added its two new northern quarters of Jdeide and Tadrib, populated especially by Christians, and remained populous and in full economic boom during the Ottoman period. Under the Ottomans, Aleppo was the third largest city of the Empire, behind only Istanbul and Cairo in terms of

Images of the citadel of Aleppo, a true masterpiece of medieval military art. The layering of various archaeological strata has permitted scholars to reconstruct the history of the city from its very beginnings.

Another interesting attraction is the **Citadel Museum**, exhibiting a collection of weapons and military engines, various objects, and antiquities unearthed during the excavation and restoration of the Aleppo citadel site.

wealth and importance. Many dozens of caravansaries and complexes of artisan workshops were built both inside and outside of the medieval walls. Tragedy struck in 1822, however, when an earthquake killed 60 percent of the population.

In the 20th century, Aleppo has been negatively affected by the French cession to Turkey of the area of Hatay—the city's natural outlet to the sea—and by a lack of investment, which flows more readily to Damascus. Nevertheless, the city is still a main center of commerce and industry.

THE CITADEL

Occupied and fortified in very remote times, the circular 55-meter high mound upon which the Citadel rises is undoubtedly the most spectacular sight in Aleppo. The complex fortified structure was built in successive phases under the Hamdanids (the first construction), Zengids (nearly complete reconstruction), Ayyubids (the moat, escarpment, the only bridge, and two towers that guard

the bridge) and Mamluks (reconstruction of the sections destroyed by the Mongols). Within the walls are numerous civil and religious structures, many of them heavily, if not irremediably, damaged by the 1822 earthquake. However, you can still visit the vestiges of a *public bath* from the 11th century, the **Great Mosque** founded in 1214 and altered several times thereafter, the **Royal Palace**, built at the end of the Ayyubid period and featuring baths and mosques, and the famous **Throne Hall**, recently restored to its late Mamluk design. Also impressive is a *walk along the walls*, which offer splendid views of the city.

Considered impossible to conquer, the Citadel constituted an extreme defensive bulwark for the entire population against external

Images of the citadel and a detail of the sumptuous Throne Room built by the Mamluk sultans and more recently redecorated.

attacks; but it was at the same time a weakness for whoever exercised authority from afar. Thus, to avoid the risk of insurrection and rebellion, at times incited by the governors of Aleppo, from the 11th century onward the Citadel had its own governor, who, although with slightly less authority, limited the power of the governor of the city.

The Great Mosque, with its elegant minaret from the Seleucid era. In the interior of the mosque, protected by a brass grating, lie the relics of Saint Zachary, father of Saint John the Baptist, which are greatly venerated by the people.

A HOTEL AND A CENTURY OF HISTORY

The rooms of the Middle East's most famous hotel have been the theater of a hundred years of history, during which the lives of three generations of the Armenian Mazloumian family have interwoven with those of the many celebrities who have been guests at the Baron, a name that means "lord" in Armenian. The 1911 inaugural ceremony was for Aleppo a society event. For construction of the hotel, an architect in great vogue at the time, Kaspar Nafilyan, was called in from Paris; from Egypt came the cement and above all the sumptuous ceramic tiles. The light blue enameled metal sign of the "Baron's Hotel" proclaimed its message in Arabic, Armenian, and English over the main entrance.

Agatha Christie stayed in room 203; her husband, Max Mallowan, was working at an archaeological site in northern Syria while she wrote *Murder on the Orient Express*; a nearby room had hosted Charles Lindbergh, whose dramatic family story was Christie's inspiration for her novel. For at least a year, room 202 was the home of Thomas Edward Lawrence before he was Lawrence of Arabia but only a young archaeologist working with the great Leonard Wolley at the Karkemish digs. Other guests have been statesmen, from De Gaulle to Churchill, and personalities from the world of culture, including the Italian writer and director Pier Paolo Pasolini, who with his troupe stayed in the hotel while shooting several scenes for his celebrated *Medea* at the citadel of Aleppo.

THE ARCHAEOLOGICAL MUSEUM

To fully understand the importance and renown of such archaeological sites as Mari, Ebla or Ugarit, as well as to have a measure of the incredible richness of the ancient and more isolated cities near the border with Turkey, a visit to the **Archaeological Museum** of Aleppo is obligatory.

Set out on two floors, the collections follow an only somewhat chronological order, with the classical and medieval archaeological finds—with the only exception of the mosaics—displayed on the top floor, while those from the 5th to the 1st millennium BC are displayed by locality on the ground floor. This leaves visitors the task of establishing parallels among objects of the same eras but from different places, while allowing them to form an overall idea of the culture that flourished in each site.

After the section dedicated to prehistoric finds is a hall dedicated to Tell Brak (where the oldest Syrian temple was uncovered, dating from the 3rd millennium BC) and to other sites of the Syrian Gezira in which terra-cotta crockery and figurines from the 5th to the 3rd millennium BC have been discovered. Next are halls exhibiting objects from Mari, Hama (Hamath in antiquity), Ugarit, Tell Halaf, Tell Arslan Tash, Tell Hajib, and Tell Ahmar. A large room, housing the finds from recent excavations in such localities as Ain Dara and Tell Shuwayra, precedes the last hall dedicated to Ebla, discovered in the 1960s and still in the process of excavation.

This celebrated statue of a goddess, dating to the 18th century BC, is from Mari. It may represent Ishtar, but in any case is considered a masterpiece of ancient Oriental sculpture. The statue stood on a pedestal in the anteroom of the Throne Room; inside the statue was installed a terracotta pipe through which ran the water that gushed from the vase the goddess holds in her hands. The robes of the goddess also evoke the aqueous element in the slight ripples of the fabric, recalling the movement of waves, and in the forms of the fish engraved on the surface.

Guardian-lion at the portal of the Temple of Dagan in Mari, made of copper plates over a wooden statue, which has now been lost. This lion, now in the Aleppo museum, was paired with another now in the Louvre Museum in Paris.

Many of the objects found in cities such as Mari, Ebla and Ugarit are enjoyable for their refined stylistic and decorative details, as well as for the extraordinary technical skill that went into producing them. The unsettling *statues in black basalt* with enormous carved white eyes found in Tell Halaf instead inspire feelings of a completely different nature, probably touching on unconscious feelings of ancestral religiousness.

The first room of the top floor contains recent discoveries from excavations at sites that were later flooded by the lake created by the large dam on the Euphrates. After is a long hall dedicated to *Greek-Roman and Byzantine finds*, including pieces of exquisite craftsmanship and a collection of glasswork of rare beauty. The hall dedicated to *objects of the Islamic period*, which boasts an interesting collection of ceramics of various origins, closes the archaeological section of the museum, which also features a permanent *collection of modern Syrian art*.

Top, a 14th-century BC gold cup from Ugarit, embossed with three registers in which rows of bulls, lions, and monsters alternate with plant motifs. Center, an elegant ivory plaque representing two rams of Amon facing each other among sacred trees; this object, with its extremely refined workmanship, clearly belies Egyptian influence. Found at the Arslan Tash archaeological site, it is one of the rich collection of ivories sculpted for the Aramaic King Hazael in the 9th century BC. Right, a statue of a court dignitary with his hands joined in prayer, again shown in the typical robes called kaunakès *by the first archaeologists to dig in Mesopotamia; the term indicates a fabric with hanging tassels or tufts worn by both men and women at the height of Sumerian civilization. Below, remains of the wooden decoration inlaid with shells that once adorned Palace G at Ebla.*

Top, a molded architectural slab (orthostat) from the 9th century
BC, depicting the Mesopotamian hero Gilgamesh with two
divinities resembling minotaurs (one is thought to be Enkidu)
and holding aloft the solar disk, symbol of the god Shamash.
Gilgamesh, two-thirds god and one-third man, Sumerian king
of the city of Uruk (in today's Iraq near the Persian Gulf) in about
2600 BC, is the signature character in Sumerian mythology.
His doings were set down in what later became known
as the Epic of Gilgamesh, the first epic poem
in human history. The most complete
version is that transcribed on eleven
clay tablets that were discovered
among the ruins of the royal library
in the palace of King Ashurbanipal
in Nineveh.
Shamash, in Sumerian Utu,
is the god of the sun and of justice;
in upper Syria, Shamash is assimilated
in the cult of Baal.
Enkidu is represented as a wild man
raised by animals.

Above, a basalt stele from the 9th century BC bearing a representation of the god Teshub, the Urrite god of the sky and storms, holding the three-pronged thunderbolt and carried on the back of the sacred bull.

Bottom, a terracotta model of a home.

Top right and bottom, facing page, examples of the statuary and sculptural decoration that make this one of Syria's richest, most interesting museums.

THE MARKETS

One of the major attractions of Aleppo is without doubt the extensive complex of covered markets located between the Antioch Gate and the Citadel.

An authentic labyrinth of lively alleys, whose particular atmosphere is in part created by the pleasant shade regularly interrupted by light coming from square openings of the cross-vaulted roof, the souk of Aleppo offers goods of all kinds set out with captivating mastery. While you might be able to resist the blocks of soap and the wads of steel wool stacked with impressive geometric precision, you will inevitably give in to the temptation of tasting the famous pistachios of Aleppo, of purchasing an embroidered tablecloth or a silk shawl—for which the city is famous—or perhaps a carpet or one of the many shining gold necklaces.

The market is located next to the area of Aleppo's most important medieval buildings, including the Great Mosque.

KHAN AL-WAZIR

This caravansary, the name of which means "Khan of the Minister," was built in 1682. One of Aleppo's most beautiful, it boasts a monumental entrance enlivened by beautiful *geometric decorative motifs* in white and black stone.

On the interior facade, two craftsmen, one Christian, one Muslim, each depicted a different motif: the first, a cross; the second, a minaret.

Today, the interior of the caravansary is a shop selling Oriental curiosities, typical crafts products, and rugs.

HAMMAM YALBOUGHA AL-NASRI

Hammam: the name alone evokes the sensual, toned-down atmospheres of Ingrès' paintings; and as Scheherazade, protagonist of the *One Thousand and One Arabian Nights*, said, "no city is complete without its Turkish bath." After the fall of the Roman Empire, the Arabs perpetuated the refined tradition of the bath, transforming it (with smaller rooms and simpler procedures) into the *hammam*, which in Arabic means "spreader of warmth." The heart of the *hammam* is the room called the *harara*, where the heat exceeds 40°C and the humidity is close to 100%. Like the Roman bath, the *hammam* had a precise social function: it was not only a place for caring for the body but also offered a pleasant, relaxing occasion for meeting and socializing. This *hammam*, in Aleppo, southeast of the bridge that leads to the citadel, was constructed in 1491.

QALAAT SAMAAN

Y ou cannot leave Aleppo without dedicating at least an afternoon to visiting the fascinating vestiges of the **early Christian complex** that was home to Saint Simeon the Stylite.

The state of conservation of these 5th-century structures, which have suffered damage wrought by, among other things, an earthquake and numerous wars, is remarkable. The complex is also striking for the originality of the layout, with *four, three-nave basilicas* branching out from a common octagonal court, now without its cupola. At the center was the column upon which Simeon lived; originally more than 15 meters high, the *column* has since been considerably reduced a piece at a time by souvenir-seeking pilgrims, so that today it is nothing more than a stump about two meters high. Its suggestiveness nonetheless remains, and it is still visible throughout the complex, as the architects of the building

The remains of the column around which the sanctuary was built in the 5th century. It was here that Saint Simeon Stylites, born in Antioch in 389, spent the last 36 years of his life, exposed to the sun and the elements, in continual mortification of the flesh, praying and preaching to the masses of pilgrims below. Simeon was the first ascetic to live on a column; the best known of his successors as pillar-hermits was Daniel. The stylite phenomenon lasted through the 12th century in the East.

On this and the following pages, images of the sanctuary, one of the most significant early Christian monuments in all of Syria due to its excellent state of preservation but above all the suggestiveness of its remains, pregnant with historical associations.

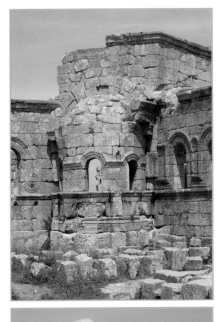

no doubt planned. The impressiveness of the sanctuary as a whole is revealed upon passing through the *portal*, to the right of which sits a small basilica and baptistery. Two hundred meters of Via Sacra led to the complex, whose *southern facade*, preceded by a triple-arched *portico*, is a masterpiece of simplicity and balance.

The decorations, sober but not austere, often feature moldings, friezes and cornices that run along the walls, following the lines of the openings.

The eye is captured by this play of lines, which contributes masterfully to avoiding the excesses of rhetorical emphasis, a risk to which the complex was exposed because of its monumental scale and the religious purpose for which it was conceived. A further lightening effect is provided by the *friezes* that decorate the tympana, arcades, and bowl-shaped vaults of the apses, with grape leaves and clusters in relief that seem imperceptibly swayed by a breeze.

Rites were observed in the eastern basilica, the only one slightly off the cruciform plan (according to some to symbolize the reclined head of Christ, and to others simply to align better to the east). Opening to the south is a *court* off which numerous structures stand, among them a *monastery* and a *funeral chapel* for monks and pilgrims who died there.

On the western side, which descends suddenly to lower land, it was necessary to lay an artificial foundation on vaults to build a basilica of the same size as the others. The loggia at its end, using an artificial terrace, perhaps echoed the narthex of the main facade, but it has since partially collapsed. The view from there is magnificent, opening over a vast horizon.

AIN DARA

Despite the beauty of the delightful Afrin River valley, there is something unsettling about the vestiges of the large **temple** of Ain Dara, built at the beginning of the 1st millennium BC on the acropolis of a yet unexcavated city that is thought by some to be *Kunulua*, the capital of the Kingdom of Pattina. The site was unknown until 1954, when the fortuitous discovery of a giant statue of a lion led to systematic excavations.

Thus there has come to light this grandiose religious structure of the Aramaic era, built in immense blocks of limestone and basalt and probably dedicated to the god Ishtar, to whom the lion was attributed. In the area around the entrance, the most suggestive section, the colossal statues of lions can now only be intuited by their enormous paws, while still legible are the *high reliefs* of lions and winged sphinxes. The temple was preceded by a paved court past which were a monumental entrance,

In these pages, details of the Ain Dara archaeological area; in particular, images of lions and the footprints at the entrance to the temple.

ante-naos, and naos, surrounded on three side by a de-ambulatory. The large entry passage is formed by basalt steps and limestone doorsills. The sills display huge *footprints*, almost a meter in length, whose function or symbolic meaning is still not clear.

The fact that there are two prints on the first sill, while the second has only the left footprint and the third, leading into the naos, has only a right footprint has led some to speculate they represented a kind of "guide" on how to perform the entry ritual.

The greater-than-human size of the prints, along with the print of a right foot found on a *plate* uncovered in the area, also opens the way to a symbolic reading, interpreted as an allusion to the presence of god in the building. It could be the god of the mountain, considered to be the lover of Ishtar and also associated with her in a basalt bas-relief found in the temple, now on display at the Aleppo museum.

THE MEDITERRANEAN COAST

Since the most remote times, numerous populations have ventured along the approximately 180 kilometers of Syria's Mediterranean coastline. Inhabited at least since the 7th millennium BC, the north coast was under the control of the urban civilization that flourished in Ugarit from at least the beginning of the 3rd millennium BC until 1200 BC, when they were swept away by the invasion of the "Sea Peoples." Subsequently, the Phoenicians, who settled on the north coast of Lebanon, built several commercial ports even further north. Under Alexander the Great, the area was home to Greek settlements, such as Laodicea, today's Latakia, which maintained its importance under the Romans and Byzantines. The entire coast was then involved in the dramatic events connected to the Crusades. In recent decades, the Syrian coastline has undergone extensive tourist and industrial development: the port of Latakia has been greatly enlarged and north of the city numerous modern and comfortable tourist resorts have been built. Similar initiatives to develop tourism have been undertaken recently in the area south of Tartus, where at times construction is halted to permit study and conservation of Phoenician finds uncovered in the area. Baniyas, the old Valénia, has instead become a center of oil refineries, as the town is linked by pipeline to the desert city of Kirkuk.

LATAKIA

Except for the fascinating **four-sided Roman arch** built during the rule of Septimus Severus (193-211), the modern city of Latakia does not show any evident traces of its most ancient past, which can however be intuited from the regular grid plan of the streets in the city center near the port. The port has been greatly modernized in recent decades and linked to the railway to allow the city to follow it true commercial vocation. Latakia, which also features a large free-trade zone, is in fact the major departure and entry point for the country's exports and imports. The city has also undergone a great deal of tourist development in recent years; dozens of modern and comfortable hotels have been built north of the city, facing wide stretches of sandy beaches. These hotels provide an excellent base for many interesting excursions to northwest Syria.

Along the coast north of Latakia, a modern complex of athletic facilities was constructed for the "Mediterranean Games" held in Latakia in 1987.

Unfortunately, the archaeological remains of what in ancient times was, with Apamea, one of the most important Greek cities in Syria are today quite scanty.

TARTUS

Founded as the city of *Antaradus* by Phoenicians who had settled on the nearby island of Arwad, the city of Tartus has maintained, and increased, its importance through the ages, today counting a population of 150,000. Its name, however, remains linked to the period of the Crusades, during which the city—called *Tortosa*—became a well-known Christian stronghold controlled by Templar knights. Protected by Frankish walls erected in the 12th and 13th centuries, Tartus managed to resist Saladin and Baybars but finally fell to Qalaun in 1291. The city has a pleasantly animated atmosphere and can boast of a monument of extraordinary interest: the **Cathedral of Our Lady of Tortosa**, a well-preserved Gothic church built at the beginning of the 13th century on the foundations of a Byzantine church. The massive *exterior*, which shows traces of fortifications added in a later period, is in sharp contrast with the elegant *interior* plan, divided into three naves by clustered pilasters. One of the pilasters is set upon a square room, which was apparently part of the Byzantine church. The room was supposed to be the chapel that, according to tradition, Saint Peter ordered built to hold a miraculous image of the Virgin painted by Saint Luke. The interior of the church, transformed into a mosque about a century ago, houses a **museum**. Among the most interesting items exhibited there are some stone sarcophagi with anthropomorphic covers, while other items range from paving stones from Neolithic times to objects from Arab times. The model of the Krak des Chavaliers is an interesting curiosity.

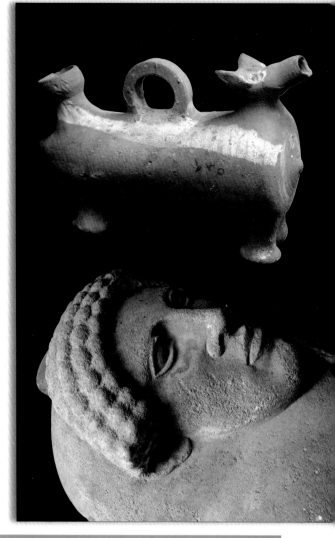

Extremely interesting finds are preserved inside the Cathedral of Our Lady of Tortosa.

UGARIT

The name of this ancient coastal settlement appears for the first time around 2400 BC in the texts of Ebla and is then subsequently cited in documents from Mari and some diplomatic letters excavated in Tell el-Amarna, the ephemeral capital of Pharaoh Akhenaton (1379-1362 BC). It was in fact between the 14th and the end of the 13th centuries BC that Ugarit—having entered for the first time under the Egyptian sphere of influence and thus no longer under that of the Hittites—enjoyed its greatest power and wealth. An indirect indication of the splendor attained by the city can be found in the letters discovered in Tell el-Amarna in which the king of Byblos, to give an idea of the wealth of the palace of Tyre, defines it as being "equal to the palace of Ugarit." From what has emerged of the excavations, begun by the French in the 1930s, it is possible to make an approximate reconstruction of the complex plan of the **Royal Palace**, made up

Left, the monumental postern gate in the city walls near the entrance to the Royal Palace (15th-13th century BC): faced as a false arch, the corbel vault construction technique is quite similar to that used in Mycenaean cities.
Bottom, a partial view of the vast archaeological area.

A corner of the Palace. The generalized use of stone
for construction makes Ugarit a singular site, different
from other Middle Eastern sites in which unbaked brick
is the most common building material. Bottom,
a mill for grinding grain in a wealthy private home,
dating to the 13th century BC.

of dozens of diplomatic rooms, courts of honor, storage
rooms, archives, and residences. Archaeological digs in
subsequent years have led to the uncovering of other
residential and administrative buildings, yielding a rich
variety of objects and tablets giving precious information about the life of the city and containing trade and
political treaties as well as works of literature that are
among the oldest in the world. In fact, the language in
which these texts are written, called "Ugaritic," is thought
to represent the oldest known alphabet. Work on deciphering the language, which took place in the 1930s, was
aided by short inscriptions found on the handles of three
axes and a *hoe* uncovered in 1929 in the *House of the
Great Priest*. Using the inscriptions as keys, researchers
were able to decipher the inscriptions on the thousands
of clay tablets found in the archives.

Being able to read the texts on the tablets, which were
found in the ovens inside of the Royal Palace, must have
been cause for great excitement to archaeologists: the
tablets contained never-dispatched pleas for help to allies
near and far in defending the city, which was sacked and
burnt by the so-called "Sea Peoples."

QALAAT SALADIN

Qalaat Saladin was the name given to the **Castle of Sahyun** (called Saône by the Crusaders) by the Syrian government in 1957 in homage to the memorable enterprise carried out by the Ayyub Sultan who conquered it in 1188. The area in which the fortress rises, strategically important since it controlled the passage that linked the Mediterranean to the Orontes valley, is naturally defended by impressive gorges. Inhabited since remotest antiquity, it was used as an outpost by the Byzantines, Arabs, and Crusaders. The Byzantine *fortifications* built at the end of the 10th century were consolidated and enlarged by the Franks, who took over the fortress at the beginning of the 12th century. The long and narrow rocky crest on which the castle is built was vulnerable only at the point where it linked with the nearby plain. It was there that the Franks dug a *moat* 130 meters long and 20 meters wide, leaving a thin *needle of stone* rising for the entire 28 meters of the moat's depth. The needle,

A view of the deep cistern, the mighty walls, and the slender rock pinnacle that supported the drawbridge. This vantage point offers a panoramic view of the striking natural beauty of this historical site.

aligned with the gate that entered the castle, served to support the drawbridge, which no longer exists. The *towers* that rise above the moat are also an impressive sight. Inside of the walls are buildings from different periods, including the spectacular *cistern*—dating to the period in which the castle was in the hands of the Hospitallers, also known as the Knights of Malta—a *mosque* with a tall minaret, and a refined complex of **baths** dating to the 13th century.

When the Saladin arrived under the castle walls, the occupying Franks had prepared to withstand a long siege. But the attackers took the castle in only three days, breaking through a weak point in the Frankish defensive system at the western end of the walls.

The Marqab fortress, built into the dark basalt rock.

QALAAT MARQAB

Built by the Arabs in 1062, the Castle of Marqab passed through several hands before taken by the Franks, who ceded it to the Hospitallers around 1180. The Hospitallers managed to resist the sieges of Saladin and to maintain control of the castle until about a century later, when Sultan Qalaun, after five weeks of siege, took the castle in 1285.

There are at least two features that make this structure, smaller and certainly in a poorer state of conservation than the Krak, unforgettable: its vicinity to the sea, which offers spectacular views, and the material used to construct the castle.

The gray basalt, rough-hewn in places, makes the castle appear exceedingly dreary; but the gray stone also highlights the contrast with the decorative elements in white calcareous stone, as seen, for example, in the collapsing single cross-vaulted corbels as well as in the beautiful gothic *door*—and the opposite stairway—which led to the **chapel**.

The present side entrance to the chapel was opened when it was converted into a mosque, as demonstrated by the *mihrab* niche that can be seen in one of the long walls. Particularly interesting are the **frescoes** recently discovered inside one of the two sacristies that used to stand next to the apse of the chapel.

The paintings of the 12 apostles probably date from the middle of the 13th century, the period in which the Bishop of Valénie (now Baniyas) took up residence in the castle.

SAFITA

All that remains of this fortress—an imposing square *tower* nearly 30 meters high—is actually the keep of the large structure that was once known as the White Castle of the Templars. Some ruins of the various structures that were once enclosed by the castle and of the wall that surrounded it lie scattered among the small houses of Safita, perched on the hill below the tower.

The village is inhabited mostly by Christians; thus, the **chapel** of the castle, which occupies the entire ground floor of the tower, has never been deconsecrated and turned into a mosque and is still used to celebrate Greek Orthodox rites. The large hall with two naves on the upper floor of the tower served as the armory and is dimly lit by light that filters through the narrow gun slits.

A small staircase on the southeast side leads to the terrace, still in part crenellated, from which you can see other castles and fortresses, including the Krak des Chevaliers, some 15 kilometers away.

The massive square tower of the Safite fortress.

KRAK DES CHEVALIERS

The first nucleus of this spectacular castle, an authentic *summa* of the characteristics of medieval fortifications, was built before the year 1000 by the Arabs in an area of great strategic importance about 50 kilometers from the city of Homs and at approximately 650 meters above sea level. Housing a garrison of Kurdish mercenaries, the castle was initially called *Husn al-Akrad* (Fortress of Kurds). Falling into Frankish hands at the beginning of the 12th century, the fortress underwent numerous modifications and enlargements and was equipped with the best defense devices for wars of siege that military engineering of the era could develop. It was with the Franks that the term "*krat*" came into use, a corruption of the original name, which then became "*krak*" by analogy with the fortress of Kerak, built by the Franks in Jordan. In the first half of the 13th century, thanks to the relative calm that characterized the life of the castle, several works of embellishment were carried out, such as the **Gothic portico** next to the banqueting hall and the so-called **Grand Master's apartment**, a cir-

The entranceway, with its stepped ramp for allowing horses to transit.

A huge water tank, fed externally by an aqueduct that channeled rainwater, was placed between the castle's two circles of walls. In this manner, water supply to the castle was ensured even when conditions became critical and especially in times of siege. The immense Krak water tank, the *bergil*, 72 meters in length, was the largest in any of the castles built by the Franks. On this page, top left, the late Gothic style gallery that precedes the Chapter Hall, decorated by master sculptors brought in from France.

cular room with a ribbed vaulted ceiling. The five elegant **mullion windows**, the first of which looks out onto the inner courtyard, with delicate floral motifs that decorate the capitals, were cleverly defined as "a smile inside of an austere monument." When they were produced, the structure had already spent the last century in the hands of the military and religious Order of the Hospitallers, who maintained control of it until 1271, the year in which it fell to the Mamluk Sultan Baybars.

This mighty fortress, overall the best preserved in the country, also impresses for the geometric rigor and the precision of the stone carvings that constitute the main architectural elements, as well as for its variety of views and perspectives. The structure has in fact a very complex plan, in which a double circle of walls encloses a moat, used as a watering trough for horses (while 21 cisterns provided water to the garrison), ramps, and walkways. The heart of the castle includes courts and open grounds on varying levels, a chapel, storerooms, vaulted halls, long and dark halls, and airy porticoes as well as particularly heavy turrets from which the defense was organized. The panoramic views that can be admired on a walk around the walls is unforgettable.

Details of the castle, including the chapel built in 1170 ca. that was later transformed into a mosque. Right, the "round table."

Lawrence of Arabia

Thomas Edward Lawrence was born in Tremadog in Wales on 16 August 1888 and died in Moreton, Dorset, on 19 May 1935 from injuries suffered in a motorcycle accident. Ned, as he was known in the family, was the second of five illegitimate children born to Baronet Thomas Robert Chapman after he abandoned his wife and daughters and his estate in Ireland for his daughters' governess Sarah Madden. The couple took the name of Lawrence. In the respectable climate of Victorian England, "Ned" Lawrence felt the burden of his illegitimate birth for his entire life.

Although he was physically unimposing (just a little over 1.65 m in height), he was strong-willed and resilient in body and spirit. As Lawrence of Arabia, T. E. Lawrence was capable of standing up to days and days of marches through the desert, on camel-back, covered with sores and suffering from fever. When he lost the first draft of his Seven Pillars of Wisdom (considered one of the literary masterpieces of the 1900s) he rewrote it in just four days at an average speed of 34,000 words per day.

He attended the City of Oxford High School for Boys and won a scholarship that permitted him to continue his studies at Jesus College, Oxford. In the college library, he read as many as six books a day; he spent his summers traveling in England and toured northern France by bicycle, visiting castles, medieval weapons collections, and cathedrals.

His in-depth study of the architecture of the Crusader castles, the subject of his thesis, inevitably led him to the Middle East and to study the Arabic language.

Thanks to a modest grant, he landed on the eastern shore of the Mediterranean in 1909, visiting first Lebanon, then Syria. His relationship with the East was extraordinary: he mingled with the local people, learned the local dialects, stayed in the locals' tents and villages, came into contact with the Bedouin world, and above all, saw the desert for the first time. He lived "as an Arab among the Arabs" and everything he learned on this trip he put to good use nine years later.

Back in England, his thesis on The Influence of the Crusades on European Military Architecture to the End of the 12th Century, based on his first-hand field research, won him a place in the archaeological expedition to the Hittite city of Karkemish on the west bank of the Euphrates organized by David Hogarth, Director of the Ashmolean Museum. In the intervals between campaigns, Lawrence toured Syria dressed as an Arab in the company of Dahoum, his water-boy (but taught photography by Lawrence), whose name meant "Dark One" although his skin was actually very light in color.

Lawrence's life in Karkemish, until 1914, was in his own words "almost perfect": he catalogued and filed archaeological finds, took photographs, and recruited workers for the digs; but at the same time continued to explore the environs of the dig: archaeologist, explorer, poet, and a bit of a secret agent. The future leader of men had already fallen in love with Arabia. In October of the same year, he enlisted in the army and was sent to Egypt with the British Intelligence Staff, where he acted as liaison between the English and the Arabs. Through subtle, patient work, Lawrence united the numerous tribes that had been lacerated and divided by centuries of local feuds and dissension. His secret dream, that of "building a new nation," meshed perfectly with the aspirations of the Arab people, and for the first time in their millennia of history the Arabs permitted an Infidel to lead them. Little Ned had become Lawrence of Arabia, "Amir Dynamite," or more simply Aurans Iblis, the "devil."

A genial strategist and skilled warrior, a great dreamer but a mediocre politician, anonymous and shabby in the sand-color English Army desert uniform but triumphant and haughty in the gold-embroidered silk robes given him by Prince Faisal, his head covered by the Bedouin kefiyah, the golden dagger at his waist. Lawrence transformed war into guerrilla, "hit and run" skirmishes in that immense desert that was his strongest ally, "because in Arabia the desert is more powerful than armies."

With Lawrence, the Arab Revolt became a political as well as a military reality, and he himself, that "magnificent leader of men," became a myth and a legend.

Palmyra

entioned for the first time in the archives of Mari in the second millennium BC, according to tradition the city of Palmyra was founded by King Solomon of Israel. The name *Palmyra* is the Greek translation of the Aramaic original *Tadmor*, which means "palm." For a long time, Palmyra was a lively stop on the caravan routes for travelers and merchants crossing the desert, so much so as to earn the nickname "bride of the desert." The city markets traded spices, precious stones and metals, and luxurious fabrics whose final destinations included Egypt, Spain, and Gallia. Palmyra reached its maximum splendor under Odaenathus and—above all—under his widow Zenobia, who was, however, defeated by Emperor Aurelian who razed the city in 272. Later, Palmyra was taken by the Arabs and sacked by Tamerlane.

THE TEMPLE OF BAAL

The Temple of Baal, at the far eastern end of the Great Colonnade, is the most important building in Palmyra. The name of Baal, in the Phoenician language, meant simply "master" or "lord": he was the most vigorous of the

The rear facade of the Temple of Baal: the columns of the colonnade encircling the temple were originally topped with gilded bronze capitals.

gods and was also known as "Cloud Rider," "All-Powerful," and "Lord of the Earth." In Greek mythology, he was associated with Kronos, the Romans' Saturn. The temple rises on a 3rd-millennium *tell* and the ruins of a temple of the Hellenistic age. Gradually, the temple precinct became an architectural complex with a courtyard and peristyle and a rectangular cella, which is still well preserved.

Construction of the temple was completed only in the mid 2nd-century AD, and its destruction began little more than a hundred years later, in 273 at the hand of Emperor Aurelian during the second conquest of the city. The *courtyard* (205 x 210 meters) was closed in by a wall, originally 11 meters in height, on the inside of which there opened porticoes with double rows of Corinthian columns. The west side, where today's entrance opens, had a single row of columns and a triple monumental arch aligned with the entrance to the central cella. *Corbels* at about half the height of the columns originally supported statues of citizens who had donated funds for construction of the temple. The *cella*, also enclosed by

Views of the monumental arch from the front and from the Great Colonnade side.

The corbels at half height on the columns originally supported statues of the financers of the temple.

a columned portico, was accessible only to the priests. Here, every year, on the day corresponding to April seventh in our calendar, the priests celebrated the ceremony in honor of the god Baal. For seven days, from the entire surrounding territory, worshippers flocked to the temple, bearing animals to be sacrificed to the god. The animals were herded into the temple through a passageway under the western side and around the cella of the temple, seven times. On the last day, after the seventh turn around the cella, the animals were led to the altar where the priests sacrificed them to Baal. As the decoration in the north chamber of the cella shows, the temple was dedicated not to Baal alone but also to Yarhibol, god of the sun, and Aglibol, goddess of the moon. The ceiling is decorated with a bas-relief of the seven planetary divinities and the signs of the zodiac.

THE MONUMENTAL ARCH

The plan of Palmyra shows an intriguing peculiarity: its principal axis (the Decumanus Maximus) is not perfectly straight but rather jogs—and the monumental arch was built in the early 3rd century AD under Septimius Severus in order to disguise the misalignment of the first and the second section of the Great Colonnade. The arch is unique in its genre, on a triangular plan: it has three supporting arches, with the two, lower, side arches facing respectively the Temple of Baal and the main boulevard of the Great Colonnade. The arch is richly decorated with motifs of acorns and oak leaves, palm trunks, and acanthus shoots.

DIOCLETIAN'S BATHS

Immediately after the Temple of Nebo, on the right side of the Great Colonnade, stand Diocletian's Baths, construction of which was completed between 292 and 303 by the last Roman governor of Syria, Sossianus Hierocles. The entrance is marked by four monolithic columns in pink granite imported from Aswan in Egypt. Of these baths there remains very little, but the ruins indicate that the layout comprised

the three areas typical of all Roman baths: the *frigidarium*, the *tepidarium*, and the *calidarium*.

The theater, with a detail of the Royal Gate.

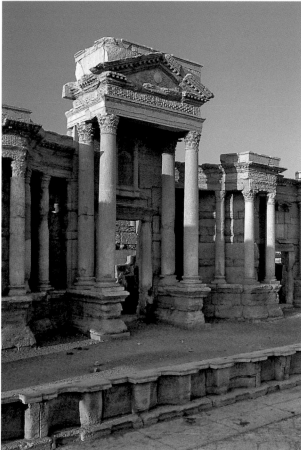

THE GREAT COLONNADE

This road cuts through Palmyra from east to west; eleven meters wide and more than one kilometer in length, it is lined with porticoes each seven meters in width. Construction of the road began in the 2nd century AD. It may be considered as consisting of three large sections. The first portion, west of the Tetrapylon, is the oldest and runs through the residential district. The central portion, dating to the early 3rd century, is the most monumental in character but was not paved in order to permit transit by camels. The third portion, the last in chronological order and never completed, led to Diocletian's Camp.

THE THEATER

An arch opening in the south portico gives access to a road that runs around the hemicycle of the theater, which historians tell us was built in the mid-2nd century AD. A vaulted passageway leads to the *orchestra* (that is, the area delimited by the tiers of the cavea). Today, only

a dozen or so tiers of seating remain, about a third of the original number. Facing the tiers rises the majestic *frons scenae*, 48 meters in length and 10.5 wide, representing the facade of a building. Today, all that remains of it is the ground floor, but it originally rose two more stories. Differently from other theaters, in which the *frons scenae* generally contained three doors, the Palmyra theater has five, the center one of which is known as the Royal Arch.

THE TETRAPYLON

The Tetrapylon, built to mask the first deviation of the Great Colonnade, rises at the center of an oval plaza. Rebuilt beginning in 1963 from various fallen elements, this

temple was square in form, composed of four pedestals on each of which the same number of pink granite columns rose to form an aedicula supporting an entablature. Each aedicula held a statue, all of which have been lost.

THE "TOMB-HOME" (or Funerary Temple)

The Funerary Temple at the western extremity of the Great Colonnade dates to the late 3rd century. It was originally preceded by a portico with six Corinthian columns and included a crypt, also now lost.

DIOCLETIAN'S CAMP

Diocletian's Camp occupies the area that was once the palace of Queen Zenobia. Under the Roman emperor, the site became a military headquarters for defending the eastern frontier of the Empire.

On the facing page, the Funerary Temple that stands at the start of the Palmyra necropolis area. On this page, the Temple of Baal Shamin, with its six-columned pronaos showing traces of corbels, and the cella, the side walls of which are decorated with pilasters and windows.

QALAAT IBN MAAN
(Arab Castle)

This citadel, which offers a magnificent view of the ruins of Palmyra, was owned by the Lebanese Emir Fakhr el-Din (1590-1635), a fierce opponent of Ottoman dominion. Finds of 12th- and 13th-century architectural elements and pottery suggest that the castle was actually built earlier in history.

Surrounded by a *moat* crossed by a bridge, the castle is circular in plan and boasts seven defensive *towers*.

THE TEMPLE OF NEBO

Nebo, or Nabu, son of the Mesopotamian god Baal Marduk, was the god of oracles, of wisdom, and of writing, and as such identified with Apollo. Construction of the temple began in the 1st century AD and was completed in the 3rd. The plan recalls the Temple of Baal, with a courtyard enclosed by walls, an inner portico, a cella raised on a podium and surrounded by a peristyle, and a monumental entrance with a columned propylaeum. Of the entire complex, all that remains is the *podium* of the sanctuary and the bases of the *columns of the portico*.

The area of Diocletian's Camp embraces other constructions from the same and earlier periods, like the Temple of the Insignia, accessed by a monumental staircase, and the Temple of Allat, of which all that is left today is the cornice of a door and several grooved columns.

THE NECROPOLIS

With its 150 ca. sepulchers, the necropolis of Palmyra is the largest in the entire Greek and Roman world and comprises both individual and collective tombs. The latter are of three types: tower tombs, hypogeum tombs, and funerary temples; in both Greek and Roman styles, the latter are the best preserved. In these tombs, the inhabitants of Palmyra were buried together with their family members: the founder of a family, often represented reclining on his sarcophagus, was interred together with his wife and children at the deepest part of the funerary chamber, while his descendants were buried along the sides of the room in funerary urns each closed with a bust of the deceased.

Below, the stucco paneled ceiling of the Tower of Elahel and, bottom left, a painting from the Tomb of the Three Brothers showing winged Victories supporting busts of the deceased. In the other images, more sculptural decorations of a funerary character.

Thanks to the abundance of statuary and the
many reliefs at the Palmyra site, on display at the
Archaeological Museum, we have a good idea
of the culture and the lifestyles of the inhabitants
of the ancient city. Typical among these
finds are the busts of sumptuously-
dressed women, which provide precious
documentation of styles in clothing,
jewelry, and hairdos and headgear.
Along with the reliefs and the funerary
stelae, the site has also yielded up a statue
of the goddess Allat, her arm raised to
brandish a lance and carrying a shield,
both now lost. In the Hellenistic and
Roman period, Allat was the most
venerated of the female divinities:
the literal translation of her name,
"al-Lat," is simply "the goddess";
she was identified with Athena
and at the same time associated
with the Syrian goddess Atargatis.

TOWARDS THE EUPHRATES

Two highways run east from Aleppo towards the *Nahr al-Furat*, the great river that was so important in the development of the Syro-Mesopotamian civilization. The northernmost road turns almost immediately towards the northeast, and meets the Euphrates about 20 kilometers south of the border with Turkey, near the Neo-Assyrian site of **Tell Ahmar**, the ancient *Kar Shalmanasar*. Found here, and at the nearby **Arslan Tash**, the ancient *Hadatu*, are extraordinary wall paintings and orthostates decorated with bas-reliefs conserved in the museum of Aleppo. The other highway runs east until suddenly bending to the southeast, running next to **Lake Assad**, created by construction of the **Tabqa Dam**. Only some monuments have been recovered from the many antique settlements that are now submerged. Prior to the flooding of the valley, there were some international efforts to excavate these sites. UNESCO was especially active, as it had been when construction of the Aswan Dam in Egypt submerged areas of cultural/historical importance.

DURA EUROPOS

As long as you avoid the hottest hours during the summer, a visit to Dura Europos will leave you enthusiastic, even if its well-known frescoes are now exhibited at the archaeological museum of Damascus.

The fame of this fortified city on the Euphrates, founded by the Macedonians on the site of an older settlement, is linked above all to a strange fate. A flourishing caravan center on the route between Mesopotamia and the Mediterranean, Dura passed to the Parthians in the 2nd century BC and was then wrested away by Trajan and the Romans, who maintained their rule until 256 AD. In that year, the Persian dynasty of the Sassanians took control of the city, suddenly spelling its demise. The absence of coins after that time has allowed researchers to date the extremely interesting **frescoes** found in some of the 16 religious buildings of Dura, an extraordinarily cosmopolitan city in which Babylonian cults coexisted with paganism, Judaism, and early Christianity.

With no subsequent cultures adding layers to the vestiges, it has been possible to uncover important clues for the understanding of these religions and in particular for reconstructing the formative stages of the universalist cults. The oldest surviving *domus ecclesiae* was found here, while in the *synagogue*, reconstructed in the museum of Damascus, the walls were decorated with figurative frescoes presumably depicting lost manuscripts of the Old Testament. In consideration of the subsequent iconoclastic rigor of Jewish art,

The Dura Europos citadel offers a sweeping panorama over the valley of the Euphrates. This site was inhabited as early as the Assyrian age and was selected as the headquarters of the first Greek garrison.

these paintings represent very important documentation and have stimulated debate on historical, iconographic, and stylistic problems.

The frescoes depicting scenes from the New Testament found in the *Christian building* are just as important, as is the "*Sacrifice of Conon*" found in the *Temple of Baal*, one of the sanctuaries built in the 1st century AD. In addition to the imposing **Palmyra Gate**, through which you enter the city, two other gates on the Euphrates side passed through the massive walls of Dura Europos, futilely rebuilt by the Romans after an earthquake struck shortly before the Sassanian attack.

Passing through a great extension of ruins, you reach the so-called **Qasr Al-Malik** (King's Castle), the most imposing structure of the city. The fortified citadel was built directly above the Euphrates and offers a magnificent view of the river.

DEIR EZ-ZOR MUSEUM

Founded in 1996 by the Freie Universität of Berlin, the Deir ez-Zor Museum is dedicated principally to finds brought to light in Jezira, the extensive region comprising the north and center of ancient Mesopotamia and which, until the Mongol invasions of the 13th century, was a melting pot for many Oriental cultures.

The collections range from remains from the Neolithic Age to the Third Millennium (including a superb *bull with a human head* from Tell Brak); from the era of Amorite domination of Mari to the period of Mitanni rule; from the neo-Assyrian to the Roman and Byzantine periods.

The Deir Ez-Zor Museum, like that of Damascus, hosts a large exhibit of statues typical of the artistic styles of ancient Syria, including the depiction of a court dignitary wearing the characteristic kaunakès, with joined hands and inlaid eyes, and a female figure wearing a flounced dress; or again, the stylized, somewhat unsettling head of a female idol. One of the museum's finest pieces is the 17th-century BC statue of Pazuru, one of the many deities that populated the religious world of the inhabitants of ancient Syria. Pazuru was an evil entity, a demon who inflicted disasters and plagues.

MARI

L aid out around a semi-circular hill that was perhaps the base of a temple or a *zikkurat* of the end of the 3rd millennium BC, the ruins of the city of Mari emerged by chance during the French protectorate period and made the fame of André Parrot, the archaeologist who initially directed the excavations.

ANDRÉ PARROT

André Parrot (Désandans 1901 - Paris 1980) was one of the world's greatest experts in Middle Eastern archaeology. He directed numerous digs in Lebanon, Iraq, and above all in Syria, where he discovered the great archaeological site of the city-state of Mari and studied it for a forty-year period between 1933 and 1974. Curator-in-Chief of the French National Museums in 1946, he also served as Director of the Louvre Museum from 1968 through 1972. His books and many other published works are considered "classics" of Sumerian archaeology.

Several images of the digs at Mari, which was immediately identified by André Parrot as the ancient site of Tell Hariri.

Since then, dozens of archaeological campaigns have uncovered one of the oldest urban settlements in the world, founded at the beginning of the 3rd millennium BC by a Semitic population of Sumerian culture and influenced by cultures from upper Syria. Destroyed by Lugalzaggisi, king of the Uruk, around 2450 BC, Mari flourished again under the Akkadians of Sargon and under the so-called *Shakkanakku*, who probably exercised power over it for the king of Ur.

The Amorites, and especially King Zimri-Lim, brought the city to a new apex of splendor in the first half of the 18th century BC, followed by another and substantially definitive episode of destruction in 1758 BC by the well-known Babylonian ruler Hammurabi.

Difficult to decipher because of the overlapping stratification of different periods, the ruins of Mari are most spectacular in and around the famous **Royal Palace**, an immense labyrinth of more than 300 rooms, some of which are five meters high. Almost entirely constructed of raw earth, the building is covered by a large protective roof that filters the blinding brightness of the sun.

HALABIJE

The twin fortresses of **Halabiye** and **Zalebiye** were built in the 3rd century AD by the Palmyrenes on opposite banks of the Euphrates, at a shallow point in the river that exposed the population of eastern Syria to invasions from Persia. Similar fears promoted the reconstruction of the walls by Emperor Justinian in the 6th century. Although the rectangular walls of Zalebiye, on the left side of the river, have weathered the passage of time better, the fortress of Halabiye is more suggestive thanks to its extraordinary dominating position on a steep rise. The plan of the nearly triangular structure is also unusual, with one side running along the bank of the river and the other two climbing suddenly towards the basalt summit where the defensive fortifications were concentrated. The *walls*, with their many square *towers*, are sometimes cut with *ogival arcades* that frame a spectacular panorama of the Euphrates and the green cultivated strip on the opposite bank. The soft light of the sunset, with its infinite variation of hues that multiply in reflections off of the river, makes the landscape particularly suggestive.

QALAAT JABER

This imposing fortress of pre-Islamic origin that dominated the river from a high plain is one of the few monuments to have actually gained by the construction of the Tabqa Dam: it is now, in fact, almost surrounded by Lake Assad, making its position still more striking.

The structure, probably built by the Seleucids and reconstructed during Abbasid times, received the name of **Qalaat Jaber** from a blind man—Jaber al-Malik an-Nimayri—of a Qashir tribe that took refuge there in the 11th century. The castle, surrounded by double ring of *walls* with some 35 towers, was built entirely in brick, often set in pleasantly geometric motifs.

The still extant *minaret* was built after the fortress had passed on to Nur al-Din, but many of the structures subsequently built by the Ayyubids suffered heavy damage at the hands of the Mongols. Restoration in 1335 was carried out personally by Tingiz, the Mamluk governor of Damascus; still today, you can find throughout the area fragments of refined ceramic crockery that was produced in the nearby city of Raqqa until the Mongol invasion. This provides some measure of the fury of the invaders, but also of the luxury that must have characterized the life of the castle before it was sieged.

Beautiful and majestic, the Qalaat Jaber fortress dominates the waters of Lake Assad.

RESAFA

In complete abandonment, the high walls that still encircle the city of **Resafa** appear suddenly on the horizon, like a mirage in the middle of this high desert that is enlivened only by an occasional Bedouin tent.

A settlement of ancient origins, the city enjoyed a remarkably flourishing period during Roman and Byzantine times. In honor of Saint Sergius, a Roman officer stationed on the Euphrates who was martyred under Diocletian, the city was rechristened *Sergiopolis* and became a popular destination for pilgrims.

Like many other settlements on the frontier, Resafa passed under diverse rulers before finally being conquered by the Arabs, who under the Umayyads built a caravansary and a palace whose ruins are still visible on a hill near the southeastern corner of the walls. For much of the Middle Ages the city continued to be a flourishing center of production and trade, until the Mamluk Sultan Baybars conquered it and decided to deport the entire population to Hama. Suddenly abandoned, the city slowly decayed beneath the sun. Many of the buildings are now reduced to piles of ruins and even those few that are partially standing, such as the suggestive *gallery* covered by barrel vaults next to the north wall, or the *church of the martyrs*, located on the cardus, show evident signs of impairment when they are not near to collapse. Still legible, however, is the structure of the **Basilica of the Holy Cross** or **Basilica of Saint Sergius**, which partially preserves the main nave and the apsidal area.

The *walls* are set in a rectangle of about 500 by 300 meters, with a fortified gate at the center of each side. Access to the ruins is through the **North Gate**, with its three arches and five arcades of extraordinary elegance, underlined by a frieze minutely sculpted according to the great Byzantine tradition of Syria. The pink stone with streaks of gypsum of the city's buildings lights up suggestively under the rays of the sun, creating an unforgettable sight.

The interior of the Basilica of the Holy Cross, in Resafa,
in which the arches of the nave are marked off by columns and supported by pillars.

BOSRA

A particular sensation awaits visitors to the town of Bosra, which conserves—even in the decoration of the *frons scenae*—an almost intact Roman theater of great proportions enclosed in a medieval fortress. The urban and monumental structures of the Roman and high medieval periods are also in a good state of conservation and are often still in use. Visitors will be impressed that one of the main streets of the town is still the basalt-fronted decumanus of the Roman city, picturesquely set amid the remains of colonnades and capitals that the townspeople put to numerous practical uses.

Already known to the Egyptians in the mid second millennium BC, Bosra went through a period of great prosperity starting in the 2nd century BC under the rule of the Nabateans, who, with the city of Petra, controlled the trans-Jordanian trade routes. Under Trajan (106 AD), Bosra became the capital of the Roman province of Arabia and was given a new urban plan and monuments, many of which still remain. Many basilicas were built in the early Christian period; while some of them are still standing, they are in need of restoration. In the early Islamic period, the caravan center of Bosra was an important stopover for pilgrims traveling to Mecca. The pilgrims, attracted by the possibility of stocking up on food and water, which was provided by the two open cisterns that still exist, also attributed another distinction to the city.

According to tradition, Bosra was where Mohammed met the Christian monk Bhira, who predicted that the young boy was destined to become the Prophet.

The steady loss of population over the centuries, starting with the Mongol invasions of the 13th century, meant there was little need to construct new buildings, typically done by recycling material from the ancient structures. Bosra therefore represents a paradox: its recent tourist development—which will presumably lead to increased economic activity—is the result of ancient monuments that have survived only thanks to the city's past socio-economic decline.

ROMAN BOSRA

As opposed to most other Middle Eastern cities that flourished during Roman times—which have grown over themselves, canceling the vestiges of the past, or else have been abandoned, perhaps after a natural disaster or war, and substituted by new adjacent settlements—Bosra presents a medieval urban fabric lying within the antique setting. Its still preserved street plan features public structures, which have rarely survived in other towns, including the **crypto-portico** (a semi-subterranean storage area, next to the forum), a **nymphaeum**, a three-vaulted monumental **arch** (3rd century), the remains of two Roman *baths*, a **tetrapylon**, and two *gates*, one of which (the eastern gate) dates back to the Nabatean era. Around the remains of the colonnades that once flanked the **Decumanus Maximus** the elderly sit to rest and watch pedestrians pass by, while children play and housewives carry wares in and out of their homes. The panels of basalt that adorn the structures of the main

Several views of the interior of the theater and one of the many Roman statues that adorned the frons scenae *and the orchestra.*

*From top to bottom, the Nabatean Gate,
a view of the Cardus Maximus, and the Nymphaeum.*

road, with its busy traffic of people and animals, are almost 2000 years old.

Dominating all of this is the large *fortress* built between the 11th and 13th centuries, which encloses, and has thus protected, the **Roman theater**. The medieval fortress, which also features 12 massive square towers and covered cross-vaulted rooms, presently houses the **Museum of Popular Art and Tradition** and the **Archaeological Museum**. The theater, whose *cavea* is more than 100 meters in diameter, appears after visitors pass through narrow passageways. Thanks to restoration carried out in the 1970s, the theater is now used for cultural events during the summer. The dimensions of the theater, whose capacity of 15,000 spectators is, respectively, five times and almost three times greater than the Jordanian theaters in Jerash and Amman, provides a useful clue about the importance of Bosra in Roman times. The presence of the Arab fortress, which tightly encloses this architectural jewel of the 2nd century AD, has allowed for the nearly intact survival of the wall of the proscenium, 45 meters wide and impressively deep. The division of the seating area into three tiers remains perfectly legible and the lowest tier, in an elegant Corinthian style, has been almost entirely preserved.

The baths, the storehouses for market goods, and the Roman cistern.

CHRISTIAN AND MUSLIM BOSRA

The medieval religious buildings of Bosra are also of great interest. Unjustly ignored are, for example, the ruins of the **Cathedral of Saints Sergius, Bacchus and Leontius**, built in 513 with an ambitious original plan that was repeated in San Vitale, in Ravenna, and in famous churches of Costantinople. The daring structural plan—based on a square hall with niches and apses and covered by a great dome set on pilasters—was still experimental and began to slip soon after its completion. Nevertheless, the vestiges of the building constitute precious testimony for the reconstruction of this phase of Christian architectural history.

The Muslim constructions of Bosra all predate 1372, the date on which the **Hammam Manjak**, or public bath, was built. The bath was recently restored and now houses a small **museum**. Facing the hamam is the **Mosque of Omar**, the oldest mosque in the city. Founded in the earliest Islamic era, the mosque was subsequently altered by the Seljuks, who added the splendid stucco frieze on the far, south-facing wall, and was then altered a second time in 1220 with the addition of the minaret.

The **Mosque of Mabrak** ("place of the kneeling")

was also built over several periods. The mosque was erected to commemorate the spot where Mohammed is said to have stopped and prayed, and is thus named because the stone in front of the niche of the *mihrab* supposedly bears the prints of the kneeling camel. The first *madrasa* (school of theology) in Syria was added to the mosque in 1136. Another building of like design is the **Madrasa al-Dabbagha**, built in 1225 near one of the great open cisterns. The cisterns, probably dating from Nabatean or Roman times, were widely used for providing water to pilgrims bound for the Arabian peninsula. Near the southernmost cistern, called **Birkat al-Hajj** (Pilgrimage Lake), is another small religious building, **Masjid Yaqut**, an oratory with a mausoleum containing the remains of its founder, who died in 1257. The structure was ordered built by the commander of the Bosra Citadel a few years before the devastating Mongol invasion, and it recalls, with its cross-vaulted ceiling, some features of modern military architecture in Syria. The other religious structures feature large, closely-placed arches supporting the roofing panels typical of the entire Hauran region. This method was developed to compensate for the lack of timber and to reduce the length of the stone panels. This is clearly exemplified in the small **Mosque of Fatima**, probably built in the Ayyubid period and the only old religious building in use at the beginning of the 20th century.

Images of several of the
principal buildings of Bosra:
the Cathedral of Saints
Sergius, Bacchus, and
Leontus, the nuns' convent,
the exterior of the Mosque
of al-Umari, and a corner
of the Palace of the Roman
Governor, traditionally called
"Trajan's Palace."

The mosaics from Shahba are among the most spectacular in all of Syrian art. The scene generally occupies the entire space; the characters are portrayed full-front with great expressive impact. The top mosaic represents Aphrodite and Ares attended by Charis, shown proffering a crown to the goddess. Also very beautiful are the mosaics of Ariadne and of Dionysus and those illustrating the myths of Orpheus and of Tethys (bottom left), in which the sea goddess wears a sea star on her forehead and fish dart through her tresses.

SHAHBA

In an oasis about 90 kilometers southeast of Damascus, Shaba was named *Philippopolis* under the Romans. Marcus Julius Philippus, or Philip the Arab in English, was born in Shahba in about 204 AD, became emperor of Rome in 244, and died in Verona in 249, perhaps in battle, perhaps assassinated by his own soldiers. Philip immediately conferred the status of "Roman colony" on his native city, dubbed it Philippopolis, and built it up as a second Rome even though on a smaller scale. In accordance with the canons of Roman city planning, Shahba was encircled by walls and adorned with palaces and temples, baths and triumphal arches, and boasted an aqueduct for water supply and a theater. The Roman villas of Shahba have yielded up splendid *mosaic floors*, now on exhibit at the Suweida museum.

SUWEIDA

This town, which flourished starting in the Nabatean era, has undergone rapid development in the last decades, which has unfortunately almost completely obliterated its antique vestiges dating back to Nabatean, Roman, and Byzantine times.

The numerous finds from the area have been collected and exhibited in a fine modern **museum**, where visitors can admire rich collections of *mosaics* and *basalt sculptures*.

These latter offer an interesting overview of the religious beliefs and figurative traditions that developed in the area: they range from Nabatean to Greek and Roman art, and then to the first examples of Christian art.

The diverse artistic conventions—undulating and softly chiaroscuro drapery or flattened, geometrically stylized surfaces—sometimes appear to be isolated, while others are blended into works that deserve careful study in order to better understand the passage from the classical world to that of late antiquity and high medieval.

Qanawat

Different from most of the basalt structures built in the region of the Hauran, which are little decorated due to the hardness of the volcanic stone, the vestiges of the Roman city of *Kanatha* now found scattered among the houses in the village of Qanawat include refined Corinthian capitals and other architectural elements sculpted in relief with extraordinary skill. The **Temple of Zeus** is in a beautiful position, located on a ridge and dominating the village below. Only six columns have survived the onslaught of construction and vegetation. The vestiges of the 4th-century **basilica**, which covered structures from previous eras, is still striking. A short distance away lie the remains of a nymphaeum, as well as some steps belonging to a small odeon.

The remains of buildings in ancient Kanatha. Even though the site is mentioned repeatedly in the Old Testament, the ruins that remain today are all from the Greek and Roman periods. In Arabic, the name means "canal," recalling the network of channels for water distribution built by the Romans to irrigate the plains on which the city stood.

INDEX

To learn more: